DON'T JUST LIE THERE, SAY SOMETHING!

by
MICHAEL PERTWEE

SAMUEL FRENCH

LONDON
NEW YORK TORONTO SYDNEY HOLLYWOOD

© 1973 BY VALERY PRODUCTIONS LTD

This play is fully protected under the copyright laws of the British Commonwealth of Nations, the United States of America, and all countries of the Berne and Universal Copyright Conventions.

All rights are strictly reserved.

It is an infringement of the copyright to give any public performance or reading of this play either in its entirety or in the form of excerpts without the prior consent of the copyright owners. No part of this publication may be transmitted, stored in a retrieval system, or reproduced in any form or by any means, electronic, mechanical, photocopying, manuscript, typescript, recording, or otherwise, without the prior permission of the copyright owners.

SAMUEL FRENCH LTD, 26 SOUTHAMPTON STREET, STRAND, LONDON WC2E 7JE, or their authorized agents, issue licences to amateurs to give performances of this play on payment of a fee. **The fee must be paid and the licence obtained before a performance is given.**

Licences are issued subject to the understanding that it shall be made clear in all advertising matter that the audience will witness an amateur performance; and that the names of the authors of the plays shall be included on all announcements and on all programmes.

The royalty fee indicated below is subject to contract and subject to variation at the sole discretion of Samuel French Ltd.

The publication of this play must not be taken to imply that it is necessarily available for performance by amateurs or professionals, either in the British Isles or overseas. Amateurs intending production must, in their own interests, make application to Samuel French Ltd or their authorized agents, for consent before starting rehearsals or booking a theatre or hall.

Basic fee for each and every
performance by amateurs   Code K
in the British Isles

In theatres or halls seating 600 or more the fee will be subject to negotiation.

In territories overseas the fee quoted above may not apply. Application must be made to our local authorized agents, or if there is no such agent, to Samuel French Ltd, London.

Applications for professional productions other than repertory should be made to CHRISTOPHER MANN LTD, 140 Park Lane, London, W.1.

ISBN 0 573 01040 4

DON'T JUST LIE THERE, SAY SOMETHING!

First presented by the Brian Rix "Theatre of Laughter" in association with Harry M. Miller at the Garrick Theatre on August 18th 1971 with the following cast of characters:

Barry Ovis, M.P.	Brian Rix
Parliamentary Under Secretary of State	
The Rt Hon. Wilfred Potts, M.P.	Leo Franklyn
Father of the House	
Jean Fenton	Deborah Grant
Sir William Mainwaring-Brown, M.P.	Alfred Marks
Minister of State for Home Affairs	
Gisele Parkyn	Joanna Lumley
Inspector Ruff	Peter Bland
Damina	Nina Thomas
Wendy	Donna Reading
A Caretaker	Michael Cronin

Directed by Wallace Douglas
Designed by Rhoda Gray

ACT I
    Scene 1   A town hall
    Scene 2   A sitting-room and bedroom in the Minister's London maisonette

ACT II   The same as Act I, Scene 2

The action is continuous

Time – the present

ACT I

Scene 1

Sodebrook Town Hall (pronounced Soadbrook)
On either side are archways, and between them a backing panelled in light oak with a list of the Mayors of Sodebrook in the centre. Above a banquette seat is a framed photograph of Her Majesty the Queen; on the other side a framed photograph of His Royal Highness the Duke of Edinburgh, hanging crooked. On the seat is an old style 75 r.p.m. record in a pink sleeve; below the photograph of the Duke is a board saying:

>   Sodebrook Town Hall
>   Coming Events
>   Tonight—Political Forum
>   Oct. 24th   R.S.P.C.A. Ball
>   Oct. 31st   Boilermakers' Rally
>   Nov. 5th   OLD COMRADES' Assn.

(NOTE: *The setting of this first scene, which is dimly lit, can be greatly simplified; the action can take place against a simple backcloth*)

The Caretaker enters with a microphone on a stand. He notices the crooked picture, puts the mike down, and straightens the picture. Then he takes the mike to the centre and places it where it will not foul the Curtain when it descends. The picture slips crooked again. He is a little cross about this, but goes to the banquette and picks up the record. He takes the record from its sleeve and exits. After a short pause the lights grow brighter and the voices of Jeannette MacDonald and Nelson Eddy singing "Sweethearts" are heard. The Caretaker returns and tests the mike by blowing on it and tapping it. It is working, so he calls up to the lime operator

Caretaker Oy, Limes. Now.

The limes come on, and he does a cutting gesture with his hands. They go off. He snaps his fingers and they come on again. He does the cutting gesture and they go off. He gives the thumbs-up sign, takes a yellow duster from his pocket and, after straightening the picture of the Duke, dusts the Duke's medals with it. Then he goes to dust the portrait of the Queen, but, before he actually touches the picture, he puts the duster back in his pocket and, taking a Union Jack from the other pocket, carefully dusts the corner of the frame

The Caretaker exits

A woman's voice is heard over the Tannoy

Voice Ladies and gentlemen, may I have your attention? Will the owner of car number CLR one-seven-two B please go to the front of the Town Hall. The car is illegally parked on a double yellow line and this place is reserved for the Chief Constable.

"Sweethearts" is resumed very briefly indeed and is cut off again abruptly

And now, ladies and gentlemen, a warm welcome for your Member of Parliament—Mr Barry Ovis.

A trumpet fanfare is heard

Barry Ovis enters through one of the archways. He approaches the mike and bows to the applause. He is thirtyish, with a moustache; honest, sincere and hard-working. He waits for the fanfare to finish

Barry Ladies and gentl . . .

The fanfare starts up again and Barry waits with a fixed smile for it to finish

Ladies and gentl . . .

The fanfare starts up again, and the picture of the Duke slips once more

Thank you. Ladies and gentlemen, friends, constituents. When I look back twenty-five years to a time when a simple plumber named Bert Ovis used to work in this town armed with a plunger and a few antiquated tools, often accompanied by a scruffy little boy, his son, I find it hard to believe that the firm which still bears that plumber's name now employs nearly two hundred people here at Sodebrook, and that same scruffy little boy should be standing here before you as your Member of Parliament and Parliamentary Under-Secretary to the Minister of State for Home Affairs. That is Britain, my friends, that is democracy. (*He waits, but nobody claps*) Thank you for your warm response. Now, before we get down to business, and since this is a non-political occasion, I would like to strike a personal note. It has been said that the two most important people in an M.P.'s life are his wife and his political agent. I am pleased to announce that, seizing the best of both worlds, I am shortly to marry the lady who has been my political agent for the past three years, Miss Jean Fenton. A big hand for a very lovely girl.

A fanfare is heard

Potts enters, giving a boxer's salute. He is old, apparently frail, somewhat ga-ga, but with occasional flashes of keen intelligence

Barry hurriedly gets him to sit on the banquette

Meanwhile Jean's face appears in the archway mouthing "I'm sorry, I couldn't stop him". She enters and goes to Barry's side

The fanfare changes to "Sweethearts". She bows nervously. Barry goes to kiss her at the same time, and winds up kissing the back of her neck. The music changes to a fanfare again, and she looks smilingly at Barry. He gestures with his right hand for her to go off, and she shakes his hand. Murmuring "No! No!", he waves her off again

Jean exits hurriedly

My fiancée was the one I kissed.
Potts I'm very glad you clarified that.
Barry Now the subject of our Political Forum this evening is the Government's new Law and Order Bill. I must emphasize that this is not a party political meeting. Both sides of the House are represented here tonight because, although we may differ on matters of detail, Government and Opposition are united in their resolve to pursue a relentless battle against the forces of corruption and disruption which threaten the very fabric of our life in Britain today. And who better to speak for the Opposition than the man who entered Parliament no less than fifty-two years ago, the man who hasn't a single enemy in politics, he's outlived them all, the Father of the House, the Right Honourable Wilfred Potts?

Potts comes to the mike beside Barry

Potts He's right, ladies and gentlemen. For the past forty years I've been making a damn nuisance of myself both inside and outside the House, and I shall continue for another forty if I'm spared. You can't tell the country to clean itself up until the Government puts its own House in order. I could tell you some things about certain members of this administration, if I cared to open my mouth . . .
Barry Now, Mr Potts, we did agree this was a non-political occasion, remember?
Potts No, I do not remember. That is one of the useful things about growing old. It's so easy to forget.
Barry You'll have your turn.
Potts Yes, after the next election. Thank you. (*He gives the victory sign and sits on the banquette again*)
Barry And now, ladies and gentlemen, I have great pleasure in presenting the man who knows more about the Law and Order Bill than anyone else in the country. The man I have the honour to be working for—the Minister of State for Home Affairs, Sir William Mainwaring-Brown. Let us show him, as only Sodebrook knows how, what we really think of him.

Barry leads the applause

The Minister enters to a fanfare. He is smooth, fortyish, and hopes he looks younger. He is beautifully tailored and has a sonorous voice which no-one loves better than he

As the Minister enters a banner descends from the flies reading: "SOD THE MINISTER OF STATE". *Potts get off his seat to see what is making the audience laugh, and laughs heartily when he reads the banner. This makes Barry turn and see it. He is appalled. The Minister reads it and looks incredulously at Barry, who runs to the archway and gestures off. The banner is jerked vigorously, and finally falls apart to reveal its full intended message:* "SODEBROOK WELCOMES THE MINISTER OF STATE". *The Minister prepares himself to speak, and Barry runs forward to put the mike at a more convenient height. The Minister takes hold of it at the join, and as he relaxes his grip it falls down. Barry hurries forward and puts it up again. The Minister takes hold of the join and is about to speak when it falls again, this time trapping his finger painfully*

Minister Finger! Finger!

Barry lifts the mike up and the Minister turns away, nursing his finger. He turns to speak again and finds that Barry has raised and locked the mike stand about two feet above his head. He stands frozen-faced behind it. Barry rushes forward and loosens the join. The mike drops straight down and bounces up and down at the bottom. The Minister bounces his head up and down, trying to keep time with it. Barry rushes forward again to adjust it

Leave it! (*He adjusts the mike himself*)

Barry moves away, gesturing to the limes. All the lights on stage dim alarmingly

Barry Oh, God! (*He calls the Caretaker on*)

The Caretaker steps just on to the stage and does his raised arm gesture

The limes come clear and strong on to the Caretaker. Both he and Barry gesture towards the Minister. The lime passes to the Minister and, without stopping, goes on to Potts, who beams and gives the Victory sign. The lime goes back again, passing the Minister and stopping between him and Barry. Then, after a pause, it goes back to the Minister and irises down small on to his midriff. The Minister looks down

Minister I find it hard to believe these good people have come here merely to see my floodlit navel.

Barry does a big circular gesture with his arms, and the iris opens and the colour wheel on the lamp goes round

Shall we dispense with both *Son et Lumière*?

Barry does a cutting gesture with his arms, and the lime goes off and the lights come up to their previous level

Well done, Tinkerbell! (*He jerks his head to Barry*)

Barry comes to the Minister to see what he wants. Angrily the Minister carries on jerking his head, and Barry goes and sits beside Potts

Act I, Scene 1

Ladies and gentlemen . . .

Potts blows his nose with a noise like a raspberry

I trust my Right Honourable friend will allow me to speak without musical accompaniment. Friends, I don't ask a great deal of life. Do you? I know all I want is a decent job, a loving wife and a settled, stable home. All right, I'm old-fashioned—if you like, a square. I abhor this so-called permissive society. I believe in the sanctity of marriage. I will spearhead the attack on the wife-swappers, the pedlars of prostitution and pornography, the long-haired publishers of obscenity and that small or shrinking army of dissident youths who, masquerading under their phoney slogans of Free Speech, still threaten to turn our streets into forums of their phoney political campaigns.

Barry Hear, hear!

Minister Some of these anarchists come from overseas to abuse our hospitality, and for them I have this clear message. (*He takes the mike from off its stand. It gives a loud bleep. He looks at it in astonishment.* NOTE: *The bleep is controlled by the actor himself*) For them I have this mess . . . (*Bleep. Very quickly*) For them I have this message. (*He smiles in relief. Bleep. The smile fades*) We don't want you here. So pi . . . (*Bleep*) pick some other country which may be more tolerant of ba . . . (*Bleep*) barbarians and saboteurs and ars . . . (*Bleep*) arsonists like yourselves. You are a lot of stupid bu . . . (*Bleep*) buffoons, so take your banners and your slogans and st . . . (*Bleep*) stay away from our shores. Why don't you fu . . . (*Bleep*) function somewhere else?

The microphone goes into a long bleep. Looking daggers at Barry, who rushes to his side, the Minister puts it back on the stand and is about to sort Barry out when the bleep stops abruptly and the strains of the National Anthem are heard. This stops him in his tracks and he comes to a very elaborate position of attention, with Barry to attention on the other side of the mike. Potts rises and comes down to one side of the stage, then stands to attention. After the music has got as far as the end of the second strain, and just as we should be mentally saying "Queen" for the second time the music switches to "Sweethearts" as—

the Curtain falls

Scene 2

The sitting-room and bedroom of the Minister's London maisonette. Evening, a few weeks later

The stage is divided equally into the two rooms. In the bedroom is a large bed, with a bedhead forming a shelf on which stands a telephone and electric lamp. There is also a chest-of-drawers with mirror. In the back wall are a window, a cupboard facing the audience with sliding door for quick access, and a small recessed staircase. The door to the sitting-room is in the dividing wall and opens into the bedroom. In the sitting-room, immediately by this door, is a cupboard. An archway leads to the main staircase, a door to the hall, and a passage to the kitchen quarters. Another door opens into the Minister's study. There are light switches just below the hall door which control the living-room lights. Another switch above the door to the bedroom on the sitting-room side also controls the living-room lights, and a third set on the side of the bedroom cupboard controls the bedroom light. The flat is lit artificially by a table lamp on the chest-of-drawers in the bedroom and the small bedhead lamp. There are brackets in the living-room and the curve of the staircase, and a lamp on the desk. A house telephone is in the living-room archway

The effect is modern and masculine. A sofa, chair, coffee-table with telephone, and desk are the only essential pieces of furniture, other than a low sideboard below the door to the bedroom which helps to indicate the dividing wall

As the CURTAIN rises the flat is empty, but very shortly Jean Fenton enters by the hall door. She switches on the sitting-room lights, switches on a portable television set below the sideboard and goes to sit in the armchair. She opens a parcel she has been carrying—it turns out to be a toast-rack. After looking at three more which are on the sofa, she puts the fourth one with them

Television Commentator The man who last month attempted to hijack a B.E.A. London to Edinburgh plane and ordered the pilot to fly to Bradford was today found unfit to plead and was ordered to be detained during Her Majesty's pleasure. The Mayor of Bradford has sent a protest to the Home Secretary saying that the verdict was an insult to his town.

The Minister enters from the hall

Minister Any news?
Jean Not yet.
Minister (*calling*) Miss Parkyn.

Miss Parkyn enters from the study. Severely dressed and coiffed, she looks, at a glance, cold, efficient and unsexy

They all listen to the broadcast. The Minister gives Miss Parkyn his briefcase and umbrella

Television Commentator The report of the Select Committee set up to study the feasibility of a high-speed monorail from Central London to London Airport is expected to be published this month. (*In a louder voice*) There is still no news of the missing Parliamentary Under-Secretary, Mr Barry Ovis, who disappeared this morning after leaving the London flat of Sir William Mainwaring-Brown, Minister of State

Act I, Scene 2

for Home Affairs, with whom he had been staying. Mr Ovis was to have been married this afternoon to Miss Jean Fenton, his political agent.

Jean bursts into tears, rises, drops the parcel paper on the floor, and rushes out of the main door

The Minister and Miss Parkyn exchange looks

Mr Ovis had been an outspoken supporter of the Government's Law and Order Bill. Earlier today Scotland Yard said the possibility that the politician had been kidnapped could not be discounted.

The Minister switches off the television set and puts it above and behind the sideboard

Minister Rubbish! Who would want to kidnap small fry like Barry Ovis?
Miss Parkyn What other explanation could there be?

Miss Parkyn exits to the study with the umbrella and case, then returns

Minister Plenty. If they were going to kidnap anyone it would be me. I'm the man everybody hates. (*Looking in the mirror above the desk*) Well, almost everybody.
Miss Parkyn That's just not true, sir.
Minister (*going to the sideboard and pouring himself a drink*) Very nice of you to say so, Miss Parkyn. You've only worked for me a few days. A year ago I was a popular figure, confidently tipped for the highest office in the land, and I mean the highest. That's all changed now, since I've become spokesman to this ridiculous morality drive.
Miss Parkyn Ridiculous? (*She goes to the armchair and, keeping her knees straight, picks up the parcel paper below it*)
Minister Don't misunderstand me. Nobody leads a more staid, moral or respectable life than myself. (*He quickly knocks the "Radio Times" off the sideboard, and, in picking it up has a good look up her skirt*)

Miss Parkyn straightens up and puts the paper in the waste-paper basket

Miss Parkyn Oh, quite so, sir.
Minister They're going about it the wrong way, taking things too far. Do you know how many prostitutes there are in London?
Miss Parkyn At the last Census, twenty thousand working in the London Metropolitan Area alone.
Minister Alone? (*He sits in the armchair*) Do you think any Law and Order Bill, however well intended, is going to make them disappear overnight?
Miss Parkyn Unlikely.
Minister Or racketeers, or student fanatics? And as official spokesman I'm made the whipping boy by everyone concerned. Crooks, frustrated foreign tourists denied their nice porno films, and by the entire youth of the country.
Miss Parkyn It's most unfair, sir.

Minister It's heartbreaking. Only last week I went down to my old school for Prize-Giving and the boys actually hissed at me. One little brute on a balcony went even further.
Miss Parkyn Only a passing phase, sir.
Minister Passing is the word. And if Barry Ovis has done a flit the P.M. is going to hold me responsible for that, too.
Miss Parkyn Why should Mr Ovis do a flit?
Minister Cold feet at the thought of marriage, perhaps, and hadn't the guts to call it off. I don't know. God knows I can't be called a snob; but in a moral crisis I back the public school man against a plumber any day.
Miss Parkyn Talking of plumbing, sir, Mr Ovis wanted you to glance at this brochure. (*She picks up a brochure from the desk*) Here.
Minister Eh?
Miss Parkyn It's for the heating and air-conditioning he's putting in your country house.
Minister I haven't time for that now. It could be financial worries, of course.
Miss Parkyn Mr Ovis? But I thought his business was flourishing.
Minister He's certainly got all the work he can handle. There is hardly an M.P. on either side of the House that doesn't have his hot air system. I think you'll find he's probably gone out on a last monstrous bender and will stagger back full of alcoholic remorse.

The doorbell rings

If that's the Press again about Barry Ovis, I can't see them. I'll miss my train.

Jean enters from the hall and comes to the Minister

Jean Mr Potts is here, Minister.
Minister Potts? Not Snoopy?
Jean Yes.
Minister What the devil does he want?
Jean He may be intending to stay. He's brought a bag.
Minister What? That's impossible. I don't put up the Opposition. Besides, he's got a perfectly good hovel in Whitechapel that he never ceases to swank about. Didn't he say what he wanted?
Jean No. I told him you were just leaving for Glasgow but he said he was sure you would spare an old man a minute.
Minister The doddering old fool! I shall have to see him, I suppose—but he's not staying.

Jean exits to the hall

Mark my words, Miss Parkyn, he's on the snoop; that enormous old conk of his fairly twitching at the thought of some scandal about Barry

Act I, Scene 2

Ovis's disappearance. He'd wallow in that. Hates my guts, when he can remember who I am. The stupid old . . .

Potts enters and makes a bee-line for the drinks, dropping his gladstone bag on the way

My dear Potty, what an unexpected pleasure!
Potts Yes, yes. Haven't much time to spare. Ah yes, that's what I needed. Don't mind if I do. (*Pouring a drink*) Tell me, how's that charming wife of yours? Still keeping her stuck down in the country with those horses of hers?
Minister She's very well, thank you.
Potts Good, good, good. Sit down, make yourself at home.
Minister This is my home, Potty. The point is, what are you doing here?
Potts None of your business, but I shall be here for at least two weeks.
Minister (*horrified*) Wha-at!
Potts (*sitting in the armchair*) I know it's a bit ritzy for the likes of me, but beggars can't be choosers. And my young granddaughter who keeps house for me has gone down to the Christian Girls' Camp at Bognor for a fortnight.
Minister I may be dense, Potty, but that doesn't explain why you chose to plonk yourself down here.
Potts Very simple. Fisher-Cavendish's gallstones.
Minister (*blankly*) Fisher-Cavendish's gallstones?
Potts Exactly. They're coming out. He'll be in the clinic for at least two weeks. And he's been kind enough to let me have the use of his flat upstairs.
Minister Oh, I see. Oh, jolly good. Whew!
Potts So I thought I'd pop in and offer my condolences about young Ovis. A nasty business. You must be very worried.
Minister Naturally—we're most concerned.
Potts More than that, I would say. By jingo, a scandal in your department would kill your Law and Order Bill; and the Government . . .

The Minister goes to Potts, raises him, and takes him up stage

Minister There's no reason to suspect a scandal of any sort. If you're quite through, Potty, I have to take the night train to Glasgow. Opening the Presbyterian Decency Congress there tomorrow morning. (*Calling*) Jean!
Potts Thank you.
Minister Mind the step.

Potts trips on the rostrum

Potts Thank you

Jean enters

Minister Will you take Mr Potts's suitcase to the lift? He's going up to the fourth floor.
Jean Yes, of course.
Potts Thank you. Thank you. What a charming child! Reminds me of my granddaughter, Enid. I'm a lost old soul without her to coddle me. She's an angel.
Minister Good night, Potty. So sorry you can't stay. You're welcome any time.
Potts Thank you. I'll remember that.

Potts and Jean exit to the hall

Minister Beware, Miss Parkyn—beneath that lost old soul lies a dotty old rattlesnake. Will you get my things together? They're in the study.
Miss Parkyn Yes, sir. And you asked me to remind you to call your wife.

Miss Parkyn exits to the study

Minister Yes. I shall do that—from the station. (*He sits in the armchair and dials a number*) One-one-four-two-three-eight-one. Hallo. Hallo... Is that you? This is me. W. No W—W—the letter that comes before X... No, no, no, not your ex. W, the letter that comes after—(*counting on his fingers*)—U... No, I know it's you. This is me, W, see?... Are you being deliberately vulgar? W for William. Oh damn and blast, now you've made me say it!... Yes, yes, of course it's me, but I thought we'd agreed not to use names on the phone, Wendy. I mean—Q. Anyway, the arrangements for tonight are as was, with one slight alteration. Come through the back way, use the service stairs. I'll tell you why when I see you... *What?* He's not, is he?... But you can't let me down now. I thought you said he wasn't due back till later on in the week. Typical selfish husband! Are you sure you can't...

Miss Parkyn enters with the briefcase, which she puts on the table

It's intolerable, sir, absolutely intolerable! I shall speak to the P.M. *personally* about this. Miss Parkyn, would you get my blue file in the pending tray. I need to take that with me.
Miss Parkyn Yes, sir.

Miss Parkyn exits to the study

Minister Thank you so much. (*Into the phone*) Sorry about that, Wendy. Parkyn, my secretary, just barged in. Look, darling, we may not be able to...

Jean enters from the hall and moves to the sideboard. Miss Parkyn enters from the study with the file, which she puts in the briefcase. She also carries her own handbag

Act I, Scene 2

It's intolerable, sir, absolutely intolerable! I shall speak to the P.M. personally about this. Good-bye, darling. Er—good-bye, Lord Darling. (*He rings off*) Blasted Home Office!

Miss Parkyn They *are* working late.

Minister Probably haven't got a home to go to. (*He rises and goes to Jean*) Cheer up, Jean. I'm sure you'll have some news soon.

Jean I don't know why you should think so, Minister, but I hope you're right.

Minister I'm positive nothing serious has happened to him. He's probably just lying unconscious in the gutter somewhere. Lock up before you go. Miss Parkyn, you may go too.

Miss Parkyn Thank you, sir. (*She gives the Minister his case and umbrella and turns to the mirror above the desk to smooth her hair*)

Minister Where are you off to tonight? Dinner with your boy-friend, eh?

Miss Parkyn I haven't got a boy-friend, sir.

Miss Parkyn exits to the hall

Minister (*following*) Really? Oh . . .

The Minister exits

After a moment a police car siren sounds outside the window. Jean goes into the bedroom, switches on the light from the cupboard switch, goes to the window and looks down. After the siren, a police whistle is blown twice. Jean closes the curtains as the doorbell rings. She leaves the bedroom and crosses the sitting-room

Jean exits to the hall. We hear the front door being opened

Ruff (*off*) I'm sorry to trouble you, miss, it's the police. May I come in?

Jean (*off*) Yes, of course.

Ruff (*off*) Thank you very much.

Jean enters, followed by Inspector Ruff. He is a laconic man, with a face that rarely betrays any emotion

Inspector Ruff, C.I.D. Have you had any disturbance?

Jean Disturbance?

Ruff Yes. A hippy character, armed with a police truncheon, climbed up the fire-escape and may be hiding in one of the flats here.

Jean No, nothing's happened. There were people all around until a few minutes ago.

Ruff Oh, that's good. I'd better check the rest of the block myself. He's a dangerous customer; escaped from custody after coshing two of my constables. Helped himself to a helmet and police cape and then ran for it. I should lock your windows.

Jean Yes, I will. Thank you for the warning.

Ruff That's all right, miss. Good night.

Ruff exits to the hall. Jean follows him

Jean Good night.

The curtains in the bedroom billow, and Barry's head, wearing a policeman's helmet, appears. Then the rest of him comes into the room. He is wearing a police cape thrown back from his shoulders, and underneath some very way-out gear with a tassel belt and three strings of beads. He is carrying a truncheon. He comes level with the mirror on the chest

Barry Oh! Oh! Oh! Bloody hell! Oh! (*He moves below the bed and drops the truncheon on it. He sees the curtains billow, then drops to his knees and crawls below the bed to the other side*)

Damina comes through the curtains. She is very young, pretty and sexy. A real scrubber. Round her neck is a chain with what looks like an oblong charm on it, but is, in fact, a camera. She comes above the bed, sees Barry's bottom, moves along the opposite side of the bed, picks up the truncheon, and gooses Barry with it

(*Rising*) You! Oh, no! Get back to your revolting party.
Damina You didn't think it was a revolting party when you stripped off and said you were Gypsy Rose Lee.
Barry I didn't know what I was doing! You people tricked me. You drugged me. You tried to make me do things I wouldn't do with my own sister. Oh, what am I saying? You—you mustn't be found here. You must go immediately.
Damina O.K. So you want me to go back down there and tell those nice policemen what you did *after* the striptease?
Barry No, no, you mustn't do that! Please—I would be ruined.

Jean enters the sitting-room and closes the door with a bang

Look out! Somebody's coming. The Minister! He mustn't find you here. Quickly, underneath here.

Barry pushes Damina under the bed and remains kneeling

Hurry, hurry!

Jean enters the bedroom

And God bless Mummy and Daddy—and please bring me a budgy for Christmas. Amen.
Jean Barry? Darling! You're back! Where the hell have you been? (*She sees the truncheon*) It was you! You're the man the police are after.
Barry (*rising*) Yes—yes, I—I—must get away from here. To—to—to—Africa to shoot lions or myself. Or—join the Foreign Legion.

Act I, Scene 2

Jean No need to panic.
Barry No need to panic! If I can't panic now when the devil can I panic? What with the Minister and the police out there and her down—her down—her down—her down—I like you with your hair down.
Jean The police have been and gone and the Minister is on his way to Glasgow. So you see we have all night to discuss why you missed our wedding, why you're dressed up like some sort of clown and why you coshed two policemen.
Barry I don't quite know where to begin.
Jean (*sitting on the end of the bed*) At the beginning.
Barry Oh . . . (*He sits down heavily beside her*)
Damina (*under the bed*) Ah.
Barry Ah.
Jean Well, I'm waiting.
Barry I received a rather odd phone call to go along to the Commons and I was walking down the street when I was suddenly stopped by this young—old woman—and a man. I thought they were admirers, like fans, you know. In fact this young, old woman said, "Up the Law and Order Bill". And the man said, "Right up!" And then I felt a jab in my arm, everything went hazy and I think I was bundled into a car.
Jean So you *were* kidnapped. What happened then?
Barry Well, I—er—I don't quite remember.

Damina pinches his thigh

Ow! (*He rubs his thigh*)
Jean Why do you keep saying "Ow!"?
Barry It—it still hurts where they jabbed me.
Jean I thought you said it was in your arm.
Barry Yes, yes, it was, but it was a very long needle.
Jean (*rising*) Barry, this is *me, Jean*.
Barry (*rising*) Yes, yes, I do remember. How do you do?
Jean Why are you lying to me? What happened to your moustache?
Barry I—I moulted. It—it—it came out in handfuls. Worry, I expect. I—I just lost it.
Jean That may not be all you've *lost*, my friend. (*She runs into the living-room, taking the truncheon*)
Barry (*following her*) Oh, Jean, Jean, please.

Damina pokes her head out from under the bed

Look—look—I'll try to explain everything in the morning. (*Switching out the bedroom light and speaking to Damina*) Now please *go*. I don't want to see you again.

Damina goes back under the bed. Barry closes the connecting door

Jean Oh!
Barry Not you! I must have time to think things over, that's all.
Jean (*throwing the truncheon on the armchair*) Think up some more lies, you mean?

The doorbell rings

Barry Nemesis! I'm done for. The police.
Jean Hide in there.

Jean bundles Barry into the cupboard and rushes off to the hall. She runs back on followed by Potts, who is in his pyjamas and dressing-gown

Danger, not a sound.
Potts There's no need to run away from me, my child. I'm no longer a menace to young ladies. Unhappily.
Jean Mr Potts, I can't imagine why you're here.
Potts Most unfortunate. I mistook my front door for the door of the loo and I've locked myself out of the flat. So I'm afraid I shall have to avail myself of Mainwaring-Brown's kind offer to spend the night here.
Jean No, no, no! There's a small guest bedroom upstairs, you know.
Potts But—but the sofa will do.
Jean No, no, no, no. (*Holding him back*) Come with me. You won't be disturbed up there.
Potts Don't you worry. Nothing disturbs me once I get my feet up.
Jean Yes, along the corridor, last door on your left.
Potts Thank you.

Potts exits upstairs

The front door bangs off

Jean Excuse me. (*She goes to the hall*) Someone else. Ah!

Ruff appears at the hall door

Ruff Oh—I didn't mean to startle you, miss.
Jean Well, you did a bit—(*moving to the cupboard*)—Inspector.
Ruff I apologize. I'm still looking for that hippy with the truncheon.
Jean Truncheon? (*She goes to the armchair, sits down, and covers the truncheon with a cushion*)
Ruff Yes. I didn't realize when I popped in just now—this is Sir William Mainwaring-Brown's flat, isn't it?
Jean That's right.
Ruff I think I'd better take a look round, if you don't mind. That hippy may have just sneaked in here somewhere. (*He goes to the cupboard*)
Jean (*screaming*) Ahhh!
Ruff (*turning from the cupboard and clutching his heart*) What is it?
Jean I think I heard a noise. (*She points to the bedroom*) Bedroom.
Ruff Right. (*He barges into the bedroom and puts the light on*) All right, young fellow, the game's up. You can come out now. (*He looks through the bedroom curtains*)

Barry comes out of the cupboard with his hands up. Jean hurriedly pushes

Act I, Scene 2

him back in. She closes the door, there is a crash, and Barry opens it, holding a very large broken jug. Jean slams the door again. It dawns on Ruff that the hippy may be under the bed, so he goes to one side and crawls under it. Damina pops out the other side and crawls over the top of the bed as Ruff crawls underneath it. As he comes out the opposite side, so she goes back under again. Ruff switches out the light and enters the sitting-room

Ruff No-one in there, miss. You're Mr Barry Ovis's fiancée, aren't you?
Jean Yes.
Ruff Mr Ovis was staying here with the Minister, wasn't he?
Jean Only for a few days. My fiancé's flat is being redecorated for us, so the Minister kindly lent him the use of that bedroom through there.
Ruff The Minister's not here, then?
Jean No. He's on his way to Glasgow on the night train.
Ruff (*pointing to the study*) What's through there, miss?
Jean The Minister's study, and a cloakroom.
Ruff We'd better look, eh? Better to be sure than sorry.

Ruff and Jean exit to the study.
The hall door opens and the Minister appears, carrying a bottle of champagne, a pot of caviar, and a bunch of red roses. He puts them all on the table, rubs his hands in anticipation, and exits to the kitchen

Minister (*as he goes; singing*)
        Sweetheart, Sweetheart, Sweetheart,
        Will you love me ever?

Ruff and Jean enter from the study

Ruff That seems to be all clear. (*He does a double take at the stuff on the table*) Wait a minute! What's this?
Jean What?
Ruff That stuff on that table wasn't there before.
Jean Yes, it was. My supper.
Ruff I'd give my oath that table was empty.
Jean No. You're seeing things.
Ruff Yes. I'm seeing things now that weren't there before. Let's take a look upstairs, shall we?
Jean Ye-es, but there *is* someone up there.
Ruff Ah-ha!
Jean Mr Potts. You know, the M.P.
Ruff What? The Right Honourable Grumbleguts?
Jean Yes. You won't disturb him, will you?
Ruff You can bank on that, miss. I don't want him helping me. Thinks he's a one man C.I.D., that one.

Ruff and Jean exit up the main stairs

Damina comes from under the bed and looks through the keyhole into the sitting-room

The Minister enters from the archway with a champagne bucket with ice in it, and an empty glass vase

Minister (*singing*) Falling in love again
  Never wanted to—

The Minister brings the vase and bucket to the table, puts the champagne into the latter, unwraps the flowers and puts them into the vase, then throws the paper into the waste-paper basket

  I can't help it!
  Falling in love again—
Ah, glasses!

The Minister exits to the study

Jean (*off*) Down here, Inspector.

Damina quickly gets back under the bed

Ruff and Jean come down the bedroom stairs

Ruff Oh, I see. We're back in the bedroom. (*Switching on the light*) I'll just take a final look through here. Just to be on the safe side. (*He goes into the sitting-room*)

Jean switches off the bedroom light and follows him

(*Freezing when he sees the table*) Now are you going to tell me that these flowers were in this vase and this champagne was in this bucket before?
Jean Yes.
Ruff I'd hate to call a nice girl like you a liar. What's back there?
Jean Kitchen.
Ruff Kitchen, eh? We'd better look.

Ruff exits to the kitchen

Jean (*hissing at the cupboard door*) What are you playing at?

Jean exits to the kitchen.
The Minister enters from the study with two glasses. He puts them down, hears Ruff's voice off and, appalled, exits in a panic to the study. Jean and Ruff enter from the kitchen

Ruff That seems to be all right, miss, though I still think there's something *fishy* about that caviar.

Act I, Scene 2

Jean No, I told you—that's my supper.
Ruff Oh, champagne and caviar?
Jean Yes, well I'm on a diet.

Ruff suddenly reacts and picks up the glasses

Ruff Your supper, miss?
Jean Yes.
Ruff Do you usually drink out of *two* glasses?
Jean Yes. I'm an alcoholic.
Ruff That settles it! There's someone else here, somewhere.

Ruff goes into the bedroom and up the stairs, followed by Jean

(*As he goes*) All right, young fellow, you can come out. I know you're here.

The Minister enters from the study and, in a panic, gathers the champagne, flowers, caviar and glasses in his arms and exits to the hall.
Potts, needing urgently to go to the loo, comes down the stairs into the sitting-room looking for the bathroom. He sees the cupboard door and opens it, to reveal Barry sitting on a low stool inside

Barry (*shrilly*) Engaged!

Potts closes the door hurriedly

Potts Why don't you lock the door, damn it!

Hopping from one foot to the other, Potts exits by the hall door

Barry comes out from the cupboard, closes the door, goes into the bedroom, runs to the side of the bed and prepares to get under it. Damina's head pops out

Barry Oh, no!
Damina It's only me.
Barry You should have gone by now! Oh, my God! (*He runs to the bedroom cupboard, opens the sliding door, and hides inside*)

Potts enters from the hall, still hopping from one foot to the other. He goes to the living-room cupboard and bangs on the door

Potts Come on! Come on! Come out and give someone else a chance. (*There is no reply, so he opens it and, as it is empty, goes inside and closes the door, greatly relieved*) Ah—ah—ah!

Ruff, followed by Jean, comes down the sitting-room stairs

Ruff Well, I can't say I'm completely happy about . . . (*Seeing the empty

table) What the devil's happened to that? (*There is a crash in the cupboard*) I see.
Jean (*loudly*) No!
Ruff Oh, yes. Come out!

Ruff flings open the cupboard door to reveal Potts standing with his back to them in a significant posture. Jean is astounded and relieved

Potts You're wasting your time. It's only a blasted broom closet. (*He displays the broken jug*) Even this bloody thing's got a hole in it.
Ruff Good heavens! It's the Right Honourable Mr Potts. I do apologize, sir.
Potts And who the devil are you?
Ruff Inspector Ruff, Scotland Yard.
Potts Oh—detective, eh?
Ruff Yes, sir.
Potts Well, get out your magnifying glass and find me the nearest bathroom, will you?
Jean Right, at the top of the stairs.
Potts I'm sick of looking for bathrooms. They've ruined my whole evening. I'm not here by accident, you know.
Ruff Is that so, sir?
Potts That certainly is that so. So I don't want your flat feet trampling all over the place interfering with my investigation.
Ruff Investigation?
Potts Private one. Into the moral behaviour of a certain cabinet minister.
Ruff If I were you, sir, I'd get a good night's sleep and forget all about the investigation.
Potts Forget it? I forget nothing. (*To Jean*) I forget where you said the bathroom was.
Jean Right, at the top of the stairs.

Potts exits upstairs

Ruff What's he on about, miss?
Jean Only where the bathrooms are. He did come here by accident. Well, Inspector, I imagine *you'll* be wanting to get on with your investigation now.
Ruff For a start I'd like to know what happened to the drinking lady's diet.
Jean I imagine Mr Potts removed it.
Ruff Yes. (*He moves to the hall door then turns*) You know, you never asked me how I got in here this time. The front door being locked and all.
Jean No. How did you?
Ruff I used these keys. (*He produces a bunch of keys*) You see, earlier this evening the police received an anonymous phone call telling us where we might find your missing fiancé.
Jean Oh, where?

Act I, Scene 2

Ruff The caller said he'd been found attending a bit of an orgy at Chelsea.
Jean Orgy?
Ruff That was the expression and they didn't exaggerate. My men raided the place and found the orgy. (*He chuckles*) Oh—shocking, shocking!
Jean And Mr Ovis?
Ruff Missed him—if he was there at all. Several got away, unfortunately. It's rather odd though, don't you think, that that hippy should have made for this building?
Jean You're not suggesting that hippy was Mr Ovis?
Ruff He didn't answer Mr Ovis's description, but these keys were found in the flat where the party took place. I don't know if Mr Ovis *was* there or not, but his keys certainly were. Good night, miss.

Ruff exits to the hall

Jean rushes to the armchair and picks up the truncheon, which she holds determinedly

Jean (*calling*) Barry! Barry Ovis!

Barry comes out of the bedroom cupboard. Damina's head pokes out from the bed

Damina Yoo-hoo!
Barry Oh, go away. (*Entering the living-room*) Yes?
Jean What the hell were you doing at an orgy on our wedding day?
Barry Orgy? Oh, it wasn't an orgy. Was it?
Jean What do you mean—"was it?" You were there, you should know.
Barry I was drugged. Can't you see, it was some diabolical plot to discredit the Government. They tipped off the police themselves, intending me to be found in an embarrassing position.
Jean What position *were* you in when the police arrived?
Barry Lying down. In a cloakroom. I'd begun to feel most peculiar. We were there when the raid started.
Jean We?
Barry Me and a—er—young person.
Jean Why don't you just say "a girl" and have done with it?
Barry Yes, it was a girl. I think. Yes. Definitely. So it happens. Female.
Jean And what were you doing with this *female*?
Barry Shaving off my moustache. I knew I would be recognized at once. I was in a panic so we had it off in ten seconds flat.

Jean gasps

My *moustache*!
Jean How did you get away from the raid?
Barry Through a window and down a drainpipe.
Jean Where did you cosh the two policemen?
Barry At the bottom of the drainpipe. With the bottom of the drainpipe.

I suppose I should really give myself up and plead I was under the influence.

Jean No. The police aren't searching for Barry Ovis as the assailant so you must look like yourself again. You need another moustache.

Barry Oh, it'll take weeks. I'm a slow grower.

Jean (*giving him the truncheon*) I'm going down to the hairdressers in the arcade.

Barry Is this the time to get your hair done?

Jean To try to buy you a false moustache, you idiot.

Barry Oh, yes. What would I do without you?

Jean What have you done without me? Did you enjoy that orgy?

Barry Oh, hardly at all!

Jean Oooh!

Jean exits hurriedly to the hall

Potts is heard singing upstairs. Barry quickly hides in the living-room cupboard

Potts enters down the stairs and comes to the cupboard

Potts What the devil did I come down for? Ah, yes.

Potts opens the cupboard door, revealing Barry standing with the truncheon and police helmet in his hand. Potts slams the door

Damned feller! Must have been eating prunes. (*Looking suspicious, he opens the door again*) Come out of there!

Barry comes nervously out

So you're a policeman, are you?

Barry looks relieved, plumps the helmet on his head, nods and does a knees bend

Ach! I told your infernal Inspector I didn't want you flat feet interfering in my investigation. However, as you're here you can help me. You know who I am?

Barry nods

So do I. That's a good start. I suppose your chief told you what I was doing here?

Barry shakes his head

Damn it! That's a pity, because the stupid ass told me to forget all about it—and I have. The plain facts are these. Someone who shall be nameless—I forget his name—told me something about someone which was really something. That certain someone was going to do something. The point is—*what* and who? You find out what it is and I'll see you're promoted to sergeant. (*He pats Barry*)

Act I, Scene 2

Barry salutes

(*Moving to the stairs*) I'm going to have a nose around.
Barry Er, sir. If a certain someone suspects you're on to something he may do nothing. So I suggest you lie low in your room and don't show your face until you get my signal.
Potts Good thinking! What signal?

Barry purses his lips and emits an inaudible whistle

But I'm right at the end of the corridor. Will I hear it?
Barry I'll know if you don't, because you won't come down.
Potts Top marks! Admirable! You'll go far, my boy, and if you don't, I'll see that you do.

Potts exits upstairs

Barry runs into the bedroom and pulls Damina from beneath the bed

Barry Come along! Enough's enough. Out of here before my fiancée gets back.
Damina Not to worry. You're off the hook now.
Barry Off what hook?
Damina Relax. Go back to your fiancée.
Barry You mean you're not going to cause any more trouble?
Damina Not for you. No.
Barry Oh, thank you, miss—er . . .
Dadmina Damina.
Barry Miss Damina. Yes. That reminds me—about the party. It's all rather hazy in my mind. Would you mind telling me—did I—er—was I . . . ?
Damina Well, you were decidedly . . .

The front door is heard to bang. Damina bundles Barry into the cupboard and goes in after him

Jean enters from the hall, runs across the sitting-room into the bedroom and drops her handbag on the bed

Jean Barry? No-one at the hairdresser's, and the street is teeming with police. (*She returns to the sitting-room*)

The cupboard door opens and Barry appears with his cape suspended over a golf-club and with Damina hidden behind it so that Jean cannot see her

Barry Hey, Toro!
Jean Have you gone mad?
Barry No, no. You've just discovered my secret. I—I want to be a matador. (*He sings to the song from "Carmen"*)
    Toreador
    Through the bloomin' door

(*He opens the bedroom door*)
Then out the window
See you no more.

Damina nips from behind the cape into the bedroom. Barry closes the door, and she nips under the bed

Jean What was that in aid of?
Barry I was just trying to cheer things up.
Jean You're still drunk.

Jean goes towards the bedroom door. He hurriedly stops her and then opens the door to make sure the room is empty

Barry All right. After you.

Jean goes into the bedroom, turns on the light, takes her bag off the bed and puts it on the chest. Barry puts the cape, helmet, truncheon and golf club into the cupboard and closes it. Then he goes to one side of the bed

Jean Now listen carefully, if you're capable. I shall have to go further afield for that moustache. The hairdresser's was closed.
Barry They all will be.
Jean There's a joke shop in Oxford Street. They may have something. Meanwhile, the best thing you can do is get out of that hideous gear and have a cold bath and try to sleep things off.

Barry takes off his belt

And don't answer the door or telephone.
Barry Right. (*He undoes and then removes his shirt. On his chest, very large and bright, is painted the naked torso and head of a very full-breasted woman*)

Jean stares and points, horrified. Barry looks over his shoulder to see what she is looking at. There is nobody, so he faces front again, and sees she is is pointing at him. He looks down, gasps in horror, then clasps his hands over the painted breasts

Don't look! Don't look! She—she—they—they—must have done it in my sleep.
Jean If that's tattooed on, chum, you've had it.
Barry Oh, yes. Yes, indeed. Marriage would be out. You couldn't live with this on top of you. (*He uncups his hands a trifle and looks at the breasts*) I mean staring at you. Oh, it's no good. I'll have to become a monk.
Jean She'd go down very well in a monastery. (*She drags her hand across the painting*) You're in luck. It's only paint. Go and have that bath, you revolting little man.
Barry Please. Try to . . .
Jean Don't touch me where you've been—I mean don't touch me until I know where you've been.

Act I, Scene 2   23

Barry Really I'm not as black as—I'm—I'm painted.
Jean Aren't you? If that girl has legs, Barry Ovis, you were painted in the nude.
Barry Legs? (*He looks down his trousers waistband. His face falls*) Whatever else she's got, she most certainly has not got legs.
Jean Oh!

Jean runs round the bed, across the sitting-room, and exits to the hall. Barry runs out after her

Barry (*as he goes*) Jean! Wait! Remember I was drunk or drugged . . .

Damina comes out from under the bed, closes the door, goes to the telephone at the head of the bed, dials a number, then sprawls on the bed waiting for her call to be answered

Damina Hallo, Johnny? . . . It's Damina. I've got to talk fast. I'm at Ovis's place where he was staying. The *Minister's flat* . . . Oh, yes. It all went wrong . . . Well, he got away before the police could catch him. But I've got something that could be a lot more interesting. The Minister's told everyone he's on the night train to Glasgow for some conference, but he's still here in London. I reckon he's planned a bit of the other here on the quiet. And I've still got the camera on me. If I could catch the Minister at it that'd be tons better than poor little Ovis for making a scandal. I'll be in touch.

A door slams off in the hall. Damina replaces the receiver and nips behind the curtains

Barry enters from the hall, switches off the sitting-room lights beside the communicating door and goes into the bedroom. He picks up his belt and shirt, and looks under the bed

Barry Are you still there? Have you gone? Thank goodness for that!

Barry switches out the bedroom light and exits up the bedroom staircase. After a pause the Minister enters from the hall with the caviar, champagne, glasses and flowers

Minister Anybody here? (*He switches on the sitting-room lights, puts the things on the table, goes to the bedroom and opens the door. Softly*) Anybody here? (*He closes the door, goes to the armchair, sits, and dials a number on the telephone*) Four-two-one-seven-seven-six-three-one-five-three-eight-four-four-nine-one-five. Seven-seven-three-one-eight-five-seven-three. One . . . Hallo, operator?

Damina creeps from behind the curtains, looks for a moment through the keyhole, then goes to the telephone by the bed and gently lifts the receiver to listen in

Forty-five, please. Bloody progress! I don't know ... Hallo, Carter? ... May I speak to my wife, please? Thank you ... Hallo? Is that my little birdie? This is your little birdie. Tweet-tweet ... Tweet tweet tweet tweet And how's Birdie? ... A little hoarse? ... Oh, you're nursing a little horse. I see. Of course, you would be ... Hurt his hoof, has he? I see. Well, I hope his little hoofy poofy soon gets better ... Where am I? I'm phoning you from the station. (*He takes a whistle from his pocket and blows it, then goes "chuff chuff chuff"*) Pardon? They don't have steam trains any more? Yes, well, St Pancras is a very old station. There's an announcement. Just a moment, dear. (*He waggles his index finger over his lips to sound like a Tannoy on a station*) "The train about to leave from platform four is the six-forty-five calling at Grantham, Leeds, and all stations to Glasgow." ... Pardon, darling? (*He stops the finger business*) Just a minute, there's a porter waving at me. (*In an Indian accent*) "Everybody stand clear on Platform five. Mind the doors on the Glasgow train. Excuse me, sir, are you going on this train?" Yes, coming, Jock. Good-bye, my dear. (*He hangs up and says in disgust*) How do you imitate a bloody diesel?

The doorbell rings. Damina goes under the bed

Aha! (*He goes to the mirror above the desk and straightens his collar and tie. Singing*) "Falling in love again" ... (*He takes a comb out of the box on the desk and combs his head, then takes an air-freshener spray from the box and gives a quick squirt around the room*)

The doorbell rings

Patience! Patience! (*By blowing into his cupped hand and breathing quickly he manages to smell his own breath. He is a little undecided, so he gives a quick squirt with the spray, bites the squirt, and bungs the spray back in the box*)

The Minister cha-cha's off to the hall.
Potts comes downstairs. He sees the champagne in the bucket

Potts Very thoughtful. (*He takes the bottle from the bucket*)

Potts exits upstairs with the champagne.
Miss Parkyn, her hair down, glasses off and looking gorgeous, enters from the hall. The Minister follows

Minister My God, Miss Parkyn, you're beautiful! Quite, quite beautiful!
Miss Parkyn You've only just noticed, sir?
Minister No. The very first moment I set eyes on you, it—it was love at first sight, Jeanette.
Miss Parkyn Gisele ..
Minister Well, what's in a name? (*With a burning look*) It's wonderful you came—but inevitable. It was the vibes, wasn't it?
Miss Parkyn What?

Act I, Scene 2

Minister Vibes. Vibrations. I look at you. You look at me—and bingo! No words, but the earth trembles.

He is about to kiss her, but she moves her head back

Miss Parkyn My father owns a sausage factory.
Minister (*put out*) Really? Fascinating! I love a banger. There's something about a pork sausage—
Miss Parkyn These are beef sausages . . .
Minister (*smoothly*)——something about a pork sausage which is *not* as good as a first-class *beef* sausage.
Miss Parkyn Daddy's been trying to get a contract to supply the army but he can't seem to meet the right . . .
Minister Say no more! He's got it! I'll call the Minister of Supply on Monday.
Miss Parkyn Oh, I didn't mean—intend . . .
Minister Please! It's high time the army had some beef put into them. (*He pulls her close again*) You *are* beautiful. I've fought against this, you know. God knows I've fought it.
Miss Parkyn Why?
Minister Because I don't play around. I haven't looked at another woman since I was married.
Miss Parkyn Really? Your sudden invitation made me wonder if someone else hadn't let you down at the last moment.
Minister No. This is the first time I have ever slipped. (*He grabs her, bends her backwards, bends over her, then seizes up and remains bent rigid, with a gasp of pain*)
Miss Parkyn What is it?
Minister I've slipped a disc.

Miss Parkyn moves away. The Minister remains like a statue in the same position

Now, don't panic.
Miss Parkyn I'm not.
Minister If you could give me a sharp chop—just there.

Miss Parkyn grimaces and punches his lower back

Aaaagh! That was a punch, not a chop. Rather higher, and with the side of the hand.

Miss Parkyn gives him a karate chop. He gives a gasp of pain, then straightens up

Ah! That's it. Good as new.
Miss Parkyn Are you sure? Perhaps we should call it a day.
Minister Most certainly not! We're going to call it a night.
Miss Parkyn (*dubiously*) Well, if you think . . .
Minister I *know*. I don't know how familiar you are with slipped discs?
Miss Parkyn I'm not.

Minister The first point is, they have nothing to do with age. Secondly, they only slip when one is in a perpendicular position. There is *absolutely* no danger when horizontal. So now we know where we lie—stand. (*He draws her to him again*) I think this is going to be the beginning of a wonderful relationship.
Miss Parkyn Do you believe in giving nice presents?
Minister You mustn't dream of buying me a present. This is as much of an honour for me as it is for you. I happen by chance to have caviar and champagne. I don't know if you're in a dreadful hurry or not.
Miss Parkyn No. But I can see you are.
Minister Really?
Miss Parkyn Now where shall we adjourn to?
Minister You're wonderful! It's the vibes again, isn't it? I thought as Barry Ovis wasn't here perhaps we could use his room in there. I'm sure he wouldn't mind, wherever he is.
Miss Parkyn Ah, now I get it.
Minister Well, not just now if you can wait until you get—get what?
Miss Parkyn I couldn't understand how a man in your position dare take such an incredible risk inviting me here at a time like this.
Minister Sheer madness, but you swept me off my feet.
Miss Parkyn Baloney. (*She enters the bedroom and switches on the light*) It's been your first chance to play around since poor Mr Ovis came to stay. (*She half closes the door behind her, or it swings to of its own accord*)
Minister Really! How can you be so unromantic? (*He looks for the champagne, thinks Miss Parkyn has taken it, and pours himself a whisky*)
Miss Parkyn You men! You're such hypocrites! (*She starts to undress*) About Daddy's sausage contract—who deals with the Navy's food supplies? (*She steps out of her dress and stands in her underwear facing the door in a provocative position*)
Minister I'll contact the Admiralty on Monday. (*He puts down his drink and enters the bedroom, still talking*) In future all naval—navel . . . (*His jaw drops when he sees her. He slams the door behind him*) Er—er . . . (*He gets his whistle out of his pocket and blows it, tries to speak but nothing happens. He starts to back out and gooses himself on the door handle. He says odd words*) Hot—off—suit—upstairs—go—dressing—hot—change. (*He enters the sitting-room slowly and with dignity, closes the door and stands stock still for a split second. Then he races across the room*)

The Minister gallops off upstairs

Shaking her head, Miss Parkyn hangs her bag and dress in the cupboard. She goes to the chest, picks Jean's bag up from it, looks at it questioningly, puts it down, sits on the bed, takes off her shoes, puts them well under the chest, then bounces on the bed to see if it is capable of any action. As she takes off her shoes, Damina's head appears from below the bed, downstage. She looks a little worried about the prospect of what lies ahead. Miss Parkyn rises, goes above the bed, pulls a strand of hair across her upper lip, says "in-

Act I, Scene 2

credible" *in imitation of the Minister, then goes to the bedroom door and opens it*

Jean enters from the hall

Miss Parkyn sees her and quickly hides in the bedroom cupboard. Jean enters the bedroom, goes to the chest, picks up her handbag

Jean Silly idiot!

Jean goes to the bedroom door, pauses, comes to a decision, and exits up the bedroom stairs.
The Minister, wearing dressing-gown and pyjamas, comes hurtling down the main stairs

The Minister pauses at the bedroom door, breathing deeply to calm himself down. He takes ice cubes from the bowl on the sideboard and holds them against the back of his neck. Then he moves to the middle of the arch and does a little knees bend—only a little one, about three inches deep. This inspires him to try a press-up, so he gets into position on the floor. He is however, unable to push himself up, so crawls out of it. He stands up and does a little shadow boxing with his hands held with fingers extended. After three or four passes his hands settle at about breast height. This brings him back to the business in hand, so he suavely enters the bedroom

Minister Hull . . . oh!

There is nobody there. It dawns on him that Miss Parkyn may be hiding behind the curtains. He coyly goes to them, when Jean's voice is heard

Jean (*off*) Who's that?
Minister (*to himself*) Jean! (*He dives for cover under the bed*)

Jean runs down the bedroom stairs, sees the room is empty, and exits to the hall

As the bedroom door closes Daminia's voice is heard from under the bed

Damina Oooh! (*She comes from under the opposite side of the bed*)

Laughing, Damina exits through the window

The Minister's head appears from under the bed

Minister Jeanette. Jeanie. Gin.
Miss Parkyn (*emerging from the cupboard*) Gisele. Please try to get it right.
Minister (*getting up*) That was a close call.
Miss Parkyn You never get a closer.
Minister What the devil was Jean doing back here?
Miss Parkyn She forgot her handbag, I think. Yes, it's gone.

Minister I say, why did you scoot from under the bed and go in the cupboard? Someone might have spotted you.
Miss Parkyn I was in the cupboard all the time.
Minister You were under the bed when I joined you.
Miss Parkyn I was not. I never went near the bed.
Minister I distinctly heard you giggle when I—and I said "tweak-tweak"...
Miss Parkyn I might have done if I'd been there, but I wasn't.
Minister One doesn't imagine things like that. (*Remembering fondly*) Not things like that, anyway.
Miss Parkyn You know, I think I will have a glass of that champagne after all.
Minister All right, sweetie. Pour it out.
Miss Parkyn Go and fetch it, then.
Minister Go and fetch ... You've already pinched it, haven't you?
Miss Parkyn Pinched it?
Minister I mean, you've already brought it in.
Miss Parkyn I have not.
Minister You must have.
Miss Parkyn Will you stop telling me I must have done things I have not done.
Minister I'd be equally grateful if you'd stop trying to persuade me I'm losing my mind.
Miss Parkyn What does that mean?
Minister That I imagine I was lying next to you under that bed, and that a bottle of champagne can walk off a coffee-table by itself.
Miss Parkyn I didn't say it walked. I just said I didn't take it.
Minister If you didn't take it and I didn't take it, what happened to it, then?
Miss Parkyn How the hell should I know? To hell with it, anyway. I'm going home.
Minister No, no! (*He stops her*) Please don't. You're so beautiful when you're angry. I'll go and get the champers.
Miss Parkyn Forget the champers.
Minister Little Gervase shall have her champers. (*Patting her bottom three times gently on the first word*) Incredible! How can I ever call you Miss Parkyn again?
Miss Parkyn At least you get that part right.
Minister Witty and beautiful! It's too much, too much. Oh, I don't know, though. (*He goes into the living-room, looking for the champagne*)

Miss Parkyn turns out the light, puts the bed covers back, gets in and, sitting up but with her breasts covered by the sheet, takes off her brassière and throws it over the bedhead. She then mimes taking off her knickers and, picking up a pair pre-set in the bed, throws them over too. She settles down into the bed

(*Calling from the living-room*) I can't see the champagne anywhere. It's incredible.

Act I, Scene 2   29

Miss Parkyn Forget the champagne, I said.
Minister All right. (*He puts out the light in the sitting-room by the main door, then opens the bedroom door*) Peep-bo!
Miss Parkyn Oh, come on.
Minister Patience.
Miss Parkyn Gisele! (*In a softer tone*) Who handles the R.A.F. food supplies?
Minister I'll call the Air Ministry on Monday.

He puts his dressing-gown on the bedroom chair and kicks off his slippers. Undoing his pyjama trousers he backs to the side of the bed, where he takes them off, keeping his bottom half covered by the sheet. He then takes off his jacket

> *As the Minister starts his backing movement Barry enters down the bedroom stairs with a towel round him. Not looking in the Minister's direction at all he sits on the opposite side of the bed, takes off the towel and then, both apparently naked, Barry and the Minister swing their legs into the bed.*
>
> *Ruff enters with a torch through the window to above the bed and switches on the bedhead light*

(*Putting his arms round Barry*) Darling!

CURTAIN

ACT II

The same. The action is continuous

As the CURTAIN *rises Barry and the Minister, bare-topped, sit up in bed staring at Ruff at the head of the bed. Of Miss Parkyn there is no sign*

Ruff Well! Well! Playing Mummies and Daddies, are we? And who's Mummy?
Minister (*wrathfully*) Who the hell are you?
Ruff Inspector Ruff, sir. C.I.D. Wait a minute! Your face is familiar.
Minister So it damn well should be!
Ruff Have you come up against me some time?
Minister Not *yet*. I am Sir William Mainwaring-Brown.
Ruff (*genuinely surprised*) Good Heavens, so you are, sir. Villains and politicians. I always get 'em mixed! I didn't recognize you in the altogether. I *am* sorry, Sir William. (*He goes to the switch by the cupboard, turns on the main bedroom lights and switches off his torch*) It is a bit dark, and quite frankly I didn't expect to find you here.
Minister And I don't expect to find detectives barging through my windows. What do you want?
Ruff I'm searching for a dangerous criminal who may be hiding somewhere in this flat.

Ruff looks hard at Barry, who remains like a statue. The Minister now also looks at Barry

Minister And who the hell are you?

Barry is struck dumb

Ruff Come, come, sir! Surely you know the young gentleman with whom you—ah—frolic in bed?
Minister I don't know him from Adam.
Ruff He's dressed rather like Adam, isn't he? (*To Barry*) Could I trouble you for your name? (*He takes out his notebook and pencil and holds them at the ready*)

Barry looks from Ruff to the Minister, and back again

Barry (*in a cracked voice*) I'm—I'm—Ovis . . .

The Minister stares, riveted. He recognizes the voice

Ruff (*staring*) Ovis? But . . .
Barry (*rising in the bed*) *Cecil* Ovis. I'm my brother—Barry's brother. Yes, that's who I am.

Act II 31

Ruff You are the missing man's brother?
Barry (*defiantly*) Yes, I am! (*He looks at the Minister almost threateningly*) Aren't I?

The Minister pauses fractionally then decides to play along

Minister Er—yes, well, er—yes.
Ruff (*grimly*) Excuse me, Minister, you just said you didn't know this man from Adam.
Minister I don't. I never do. Adam is the *other* brother.
Ruff Is Adam here, too, sir?
Minister Yes. } *Speaking*
Barry No. } *together*
Minister No. } *Speaking*
Barry Yes. } *together*
Minister No. } *Speaking*
Barry } *together*
Ruff (*to Barry*) And where do you come from, sir?
Barry Yes.
Ruff Yes, where?
Barry Where?
Minister Australia.
Barry Australia. Ar, begorrah! Begorrah!
Minister Cedric flew in this morning. Heard the news about his brother Barry on his arrival.
Ruff Who's Cedric?
Minister (*pointing to Barry*) Him.
Ruff He said his name was Cecil.
Minister That's right. Didn't you say Cecil?
Ruff I said Cecil but *you* said Cedric.
Minister You must have misheard me. I distinctly said—(*mumbling*)—Cysilsozzle.
Ruff (*to Barry*) So you flew here from Australia, sir?
Barry (*Australian-ish*) Too right.
Ruff And when you got here you came to this flat because you were worried about your missing brother?
Barry Too right.
Ruff And on your arrival here took off your clothes and popped into bed with the Minister?
Barry Too r . . . wrong. I . . .
Ruff Go on, sir. Have a go.
Barry Well, I wasn't feeling very fair dinkum; in fact I was very poor dinkum, and—um . . . (*He flounders to a halt and looks at the Minister*)
Minister So, I naturally—I—I offered him a bed.
Barry That's right. Too right.
Ruff I'm not so much interested in the offer of a bed as to why you land up starkers in the *same* bed.
Barry (*stumped*) That's simply explained—er—sport.
Ruff Simply explain then, cobber.

Barry (*desperately*) Well, you see, I'd wet the bed he offered me.
Ruff (*jolted*) Eh?
Barry The hot-water bottle. It leaked. So I came down here to have a nap in my bed—my brother's bed, because I thought it would be empty, him being missing, the poor old gringo-dingo—dingbat—wombat.
Ruff But the bed wasn't empty, was it? I mean, Sir William was here, also stripped to the buff. (*To the Minister*) I thought your bedroom was upstairs, Sir William?
Minister Yes, quite, yes, and if you are wondering why I wasn't using it, my hot-water bottle leaked too.
Ruff What a small world!
Minister Isn't it?
Ruff Just one other little query . . .
Minister (*loudly*) No! No little queries at all. You have absolutely no legal right to pester us with questions. There is no criminal here and we are committing no criminal act, so kindly leave us to get on—(*he does not know how to finish it*)—to get at—leave us immediately, if not sooner.

At this moment Miss Parkyn gives an audible sneeze beneath the sheets

(*Hopefully*) Atishoo! A-choo!
Barry A-choo!
Minister What *is* the pollen count today? A-choo!
Ruff I don't want to worry you, gentlemen, but I have a distinct feeling old Adam might be in bed with you.
Minister You must be joking.
Ruff I rarely joke, sir. Suppose we look?
Minister There's no need for that. That's Tibbs, my pussy. Down, boy, down! Good night, Inspector.
Ruff I can't force you, Sir William, but I warn you I shall feel bound to report both the circumstances in which I found you and your extremely uncooperative attitude towards my search for a dangerous criminal.
Minister You will regret this intrusion into my privacy.
Ruff I dare say, sir; but I'd still like to see Tibbs. I'm very fond of pussies.
Miss Parkyn *Atishoo!!* (*She emerges—so far, only her head*)
Ruff Well, well! One of the long-haired brigade! And what is your name, young feller? Adam?

Miss Parkyn comes further out into a semi-sitting position, hands cupped modestly over her breasts. There can be no doubt about her sex now

Beg pardon! If it isn't Eve.

The Minister puts his index finger over his nipples. Barry raises the sheet over his

Hear no evil, see no evil and speak no evil. Well, sir, this is getting better and better or worse and worse depending on where you're lying, and to whom.

Act II

Minister There is a perfectly simple explanation of this lady's presence here.
Barry Yes!
Minister Which, since she has nothing to do with me, Mr Ovis will give you now.
Barry (*shocked*) Oh! You—er—really want to know?
Ruff I would like to keep abreast of the situation.
Barry (*floundering*) Oh, well, this is Miss Par . . .
Minister Atishoo! Come on, old man! Nothing to be ashamed of. (*To Ruff*) This is Monica Ovis who accompanied her husband from down under. Isn't that right, Cyril?
Barry Cecil, yes.
Ruff Your wife, sir?
Barry Er, yes, it's her first trip from down under.

Miss Parkyn slowly recedes from view again

Ruff She seems to be goin' back there.
Barry She's very shy. We don't see many strange cobblers—cobbers—on the tundra.
Minister *Outback.*
Barry Many strange outbacks on the tundra.
Ruff I suggest we all get out from down under and adjourn outback to the other room.
Minister Splendid. We'll follow you.
Ruff No, sir. I'll follow you.
Minister Ah. That makes it a bit awkward.

Barry takes a pillow and pushes it beneath the bedclothes. He makes strange contortions throughout the ensuing dialogue. Also beneath the bedclothes the Minister and Miss Parkyn struggle for possession of the Minister's pyjamas

Ruff Well, now who's going to start the ball rolling?
Minister Go inside and help yourself to a drink, Inspector.
Ruff Not on duty, thank you. (*He switches on the sitting-room lights and waits by the centre door*)

Barry makes some move beneath the bedclothes which causes Miss Parkyn to dart him a hostile look

Barry I'm terribly sorry. I thought it was mine.
Minister (*coldly*) Actually, it was mine.

Barry now gets out of bed. He has pulled on a pillow-case, open at both ends. The top is so large he has to hold it round his middle, but the hole at the bottom is so small he has to waddle like a duck. He fails to climb the step and has to take a running jump at it. He waddles into the sitting-room and collapses into a chair. Miss Parkyn now emerges. She is wearing nothing except the Minister's pyjama bottoms, pulled up over her bosom to maintain a standard of decency. Bending almost double, she walks past Ruff into the sitting-room. Barry politely tries to rise, but she waves him down and sits on the sofa. The

Minister emerges, wearing his pyjama tops only, so that he has to crouch low and pull them down to preserve decency on his side. He moves in a knees-bent attitude to Ruff, then veers right round the bed and puts on his dressing-gown by the chair. He straightens up and goes above the bed to Ruff, at which point he coughs politely and enters the living-room. Ruff puts out the bedroom light, closes the door, and follows the Minister

Ruff I apologize, Sir William, but I understood you were on your way to Glasgow?
Minister Quite—er—yes. I forgot my wallet so came back and found my dearest and lifelong chum—old thingummy—here at the door with his lady wife. So I asked them in and decided to take the morning plane.
Ruff I see, and you all went to bed at (*looking at his watch*)—seven o'clock?
Minister Well—(*indicating Barry*)—old—um . . .
Ruff (*consulting his notebook*) Cecil, sir.
Minister Cecil and his wife Mona . . .
Ruff Monica.
Minister (*coldly*) I call her Mona for short.
Ruff But not for long, I feel.
Minister Very good!
Ruff However, the reason everyone popped into bed?
Minister Well, old Cecil and Monica were rather whacked coming from . . . (*He pauses*)

Ruff shows him the notebook

Australia . . .
Barry Oh, yes, absolutely whacko-bluey.
Ruff (*to Barry*) Do you go in for rearing in those parts, sir?
Barry Pardon?
Ruff *Sheep* in Australia.
Barry Oh, yes! Wool and roast lamb and cutlets. You name it. We rear it.
Ruff H'm, big man. How many head have you got?
Barry If you're going to be rude . . .
Ruff *Sheep*.
Barry Oh, sheep! Oh! Tons. Sheep and lamb and ewes and rams. You name it, we've made it. Bonanza!
Ruff Bonzer.
Barry Bonzer, then.
Ruff Where?
Barry (*with a Texan accent*) In the old corral, nibbling grass.
Ruff (*patiently*) No, sir, where—in Australia?
Barry Do you know Alice Springs?
Ruff Do I know Alice Springs? My brother lives there . . .
Barry It isn't there. Do you know Gladys Springs?
Ruff No, sir.
Barry That's where we are.
Ruff (*making a note*) And where's that near?

Act II

Barry Ethel Springs.
Ruff (*still noting*) Remarkable number of female springs.
Barry Too right! Things are really jumping there. Ha! Ha!

Barry looks at the Minister, who gives him a look of bleak contempt

Ruff Very well, sir, what is the nearest big town?
Barry Ada Leaps.

Ruff solemnly notes, then turns to Miss Parkyn

Ruff Where did you two meet—Monica Jerks?

Miss Parkyn, we see, is quietly enjoying everybody's discomfiture

Miss Parkyn No—Fiona Falls. It was love at first sight. He looked at me and said "Baa-aaa", and I was his.
Ruff I'm sure he's a lamb.
Minister (*hastily*) Miss Parkyn, go and get some clothes on.
Ruff (*quickly*) What did you say?
Barry (*loudly*) He said, "Missus, you must be parky, go and get some clothes on."

Miss Parkyn goes to the bedroom, where she tidies the bed and gets her clothes together

Minister (*helping Barry up*) You'd better get something else on, too. You must be feeling pretty chilly down under. (*Hissing*) You'll have some explaining to do later.

Barry draws near to him, whispering urgently

Barry I've got to warn you, you've got an enemy in the flat . . .
Minister (*viciously*) So have you. Me.

The Minister pushes Barry into the bedroom and returns to Ruff

> *During the ensuing dialogue Barry takes his dressing-gown and pyjamas from the cupboard and exits up the bedroom stairs, leaving Miss Parkyn alone in the bedroom*

Ruff Sir William, now that we're alone, I feel you should know that the police raided a very wild party in Chelsea this evening, following an anonymous tip that Mr Barry Ovis would be found takin' part in it.
Minister (*genuinely surprised*) Barry Ovis at a wild party? You mean girls and things like that?
Ruff There were plenty of girls, sir, yes.
Minister He doesn't know one end of a woman from the other.
Ruff I wasn't there, sir, but he may have learned this afternoon.
Minister He wasn't found there—was he?
Ruff No, he wasn't, but his keys were. Unfortunately, several got away, including a character who coshed two of my constables and was last seen climbing up the fire-escape into this building.

Minister (*genuinely shaken*) Ovis? I can't believe it. Where did this happen, then?
Ruff A room above Plummers Club in the King's Road, sir.
Minister Plummers! That probably accounts for it. He went there by mistake.
Ruff (*blankly*) Sir?
Minister Private joke. Ovis comes from a long line of plumbers.
Ruff (*unsmiling*) No, sir, the club is Plummers. P.L.U.M.M.E.R.S. not P.L.U.M.B.E.R.S. I suppose you realize that this business must have been a deliberate attempt to discredit the Government? (*With a hint of warning*) It does show how carefully one has to behave—even on one's own doorstep. Good night, sir.

Ruff nods and exits to the hall. The front door bangs

The Minister runs to the bedroom and puts on the light

Minister I say, you are never going to believe this, but Ovis has been at some sort of orgy.
Miss Parkyn Good heavens! Where?
Minister A club called Plummers in Chelsea. I'm going to find out about this. Where is he?
Miss Parkyn He went upstairs.
Minister Right.

The Minister exits up the bedroom stairs.
Almost simultaneously, Barry enters down the main stairs. He wears a dressing-gown and pyjamas

Miss Parkyn comes out of the bedroom, meeting Barry below the cupboard

Barry Oh, Miss Parkyn. I'm sorry you've had to get involved in my misfortunes.
Miss Parkyn Forget it! Listen, the Big Chief is searching for you to grill you about the Plummers business.
Barry (*astonished*) Now? I'd have thought we had more urgent business to discuss. (*He turns to the desk*) Hasn't he read my brochure?
Miss Parkyn (*incredulously*) You have a *brochure* for that, too?
Barry (*nodding*) Yes. It's all there in black and white—with illustrations.
Miss Parkyn Quelle delicatesse!

Miss Parkyn laughs and exits to the study

Barry Here is the brochure.

The Minister comes down the main stairs

It describes the entire heating and air-conditioning.

Act II

Minister (*loudly*) Ovis, here, here, here. I want all the gen—but all the gen—about Plummers.
Barry If you think this is the time and place...
Minister I most certainly do, yes.
Barry What exactly do you want to know? There are so many aspects...
Minister Everything. I hasten to say mine is a purely technical interest. I have no wish to participate in any way.
Barry You are a bit old...
Minister (*frostily*) Steady! I'm not that much older than you.
Barry Quite, but do remember I started as a boy.
Minister (*impatiently*) Well, who didn't? (*He sits in the armchair*) That doesn't count. I want to hear more about this mass effort.

Despite his initial hesitancy, we see Barry gradually warming to his pet subject

Barry The simple answer is teamwork. The day of one man and his mate is a thing of the past.
Minister For some, it seems. (*He lights a cigar at the low sideboard*)
Barry The whole success of any sizeable operation is an experienced team, all pulling together.
Minister At the same time?
Barry Naturally, everyone has his own different talents. You'd be staggered if you ever knew how many...
Minister Go ahead and stagger me.
Barry It'll probably seem like double dutch to you. But there's Fred with his Bossing Stick; Jim with his reliable old Plugging Tool; Harry who goes in for Butt Welding——

The Minister grimaces

——and Sidney who concentrates on the Stuffing Box...
Minister (*appalled*) Stuffing Box? What hideosity is that?
Barry You'd have to see it yourself to understand; but it's in constant need of adjustment. You see, grit is the main trouble. You first have to remove the crutch, which you do by means of a sharp blow with a wooden hammer...

The Minister winces as if kicked below the belt, and waves his hands

Minister Let's skip the Stuffing Box, shall we? What else is there?
Barry One could go on for ever. Bill with the male and female connections; George on expansion and contraction and Charlie the expert on strengthening joints...

The Minister beckons to Barry, who moves closer to him

Minister Tell me more about Charlie.
Barry (*with a fond smile*) Old Charlie can give you a three-way joint that'll last you a lifetime.
Minister A lifetime? I shall have to meet Charlie one of these days. Tell me frankly, Ovis, how did you start in all this?

Barry Watching my father.
Minister (*genuinely shocked*) Watching him? You mean, like, actually —*watching*?
Barry Oh, yes, every day for hours and hours.
Minister He sounds a busy fellow.
Barry He was. Sometimes he'd be at it until three or four in the morning. (*Sadly*) It killed him in the end.
Minister That's sick! Absolutely sick!
Barry I remember the first thing that fascinated me. You see, Father had this simply enormous plunger . . .
Minister *Stop!!* Stop. (*He controls himself*) I thought I had a strong stomach, but this is too much.
Barry I don't understand.
Minister You wouldn't. You're a freak. Let's close the subject, shall we?
Barry Yes, I think we should. I've something far more important. I have a confession to make.
Minister *Another?*
Barry I just took part in an orgy.
Minister (*blankly*) I know that, don't I?
Barry (*startled*) You do?
Minister You've been telling me all about it for the past five minutes.
Barry No, I haven't.
Minister Yes, *you have*! I asked for details and you gave them to me—and revolting it was, too.
Barry (*bringing the brochure from the desk*) You asked for some gen on the modern heating installation and here it is.
Minister (*hitting the brochure to the floor*) *Heating!* Do you think I want to talk about bloody plumbing, after the disgusting things you've been up to?
Barry (*struggling clear*) You're a fine one to talk! What were *you* doing in my bed with your secretary?
Minister (*after a fractional pause*) There is a perfectly simple explanation for Miss Parkyn's position in that bed.
Barry Some position! All right, what?

Miss Parkyn enters from the study, dressed again and carrying the pyjama bottoms

Minister Which I shall give you in my own good time. I should now be obliged if you would leave this infinitely respectable young lady and me alone.
Barry (*picking up the brochure*) All right. While you're cooking up some story—I'm going to get some food. I haven't eaten all day.

Barry exits to the kitchen

Miss Parkyn How was the orgy talk?
Minister Worrying. You'll have to beat it. (*He puts his cigar in the ashtray*

Act II

Miss Parkyn Oh gosh, I didn't bring my whip!
Minister Don't be flippant. We're in dead trouble.
Miss Parkyn (*giggling*) *We?*
Minister All right. Me. That little swine is in a position to blackmail me and he knows it. You'll have to go home.
Miss Parkyn Well, how can I? You've married me off to him. I mean, suppose that detective comes back? Look pretty odd if Monica leaves Cecil and goes home to Ebury Street instead of Gladys Springs.

There is a loud peal of thunder

Anyway, I'm not toiling out in that frightful weather.
Minister No, I suppose you'll have to stay. I must convince Barry Ovis that your presence here is entirely innocent.
Miss Parkyn That should test even your powers of invention!
Minister (*extemporizing*) I know. We were working late. You suffer from a serious recurring illness and were taken ill. So I undressed you and put you to bed.
Miss Parkyn Question. What were you doing in bed with me?
Minister Hell! Yes, what? I have it! I was giving you the kiss of life.
Miss Parkyn Surely one doesn't strip off to give the kiss of life?
Minister *I* do. I find it very hot work.
Miss Parkyn He'll never fall for it.
Minister You want to bet? This is the man who thought the Kama Sutra was an Indian recipe book.
Miss Parkyn I suppose it is, in a way.
Minister But not to send to his mother at Christmas.
Miss Parkyn All right. So what dread disease have I got?
Minister Haven't a clue. I turned down Minister of Health; but I have a medical encyclopedia in there. (*He indicates the study*) I'll look something up. Meanwhile why don't you just go upstairs and wait for me?
Miss Parkyn You're not still seriously thinking of . . .
Minister Mmmm?
Miss Parkyn Tell me, now we're in the Common Market, does Britain supply any food for the Market Headquarters?
Minister (*wincing*) Message received. In future it will be bangers with brussels sprouts.

He gives her a hug

Potts, in a dressing-gown, comes downstairs carrying the bottle of champagne. He enters the archway and sees the Minister and Miss Parkyn, who do not see him. His eyes light up. He rubs his hands together triumphantly and exits to the hall

You know, for the first time in my life I was really rattled tonight, but I think we're gradually getting into the clear.
Miss Parkyn I must say you have plenty of nerve.
Minister You get nowhere in politics without taking risks. Up you go. (*Patting her bottom*) I'll do my medical research.

Miss Parkyn exits upstairs. The Minister goes into his study. Potts enters from the hall, still carrying the bottle. He looks most alert. He stands by the cupboard, looking this way and that

The front door slams. Potts hears this and darts into the cupboard, pulling the door almost shut behind him

Wendy puts her head through the door from the hall. She is a delicious blonde in her twenties—volatile, emotional, not over-bright. She wears a wedding-ring. She has a raincoat round her shoulders and a very small black vanity bag with sufficient for one night's romantic needs. She also carries a front door key, which she puts on the desk

Wendy (*softly*) Billy-willy? W? (*She looks round, picks up the still burning stub of the Minister's cigar, and smiles contentedly, as if to say "He's here". Then she enters the bedroom, closing the door behind her*)

Potts emerges briefly from the cupboard and rubs his hands together. In the bedroom Wendy takes off her raincoat, unzips her hot pants and steps out of them

Jean enters from the hall. She has been out without a coat and is absolutely soaking wet. She carries a brown paper bag. She looks as miserable as only a really soaking girl can be. She goes to the mirror and takes from the bag a moustache. She is obviously worried that the rain may have damaged it. To test this, she sticks it on her upper lip and looks at it, then moves below the cupboard.

Miss Parkyn enters down the main stairs. She has undressed again, and wears only a robe over her underwear

Seeing Jean, Miss Parkyn gives an involuntary gasp. Jean whirls round. Both stand transfixed

Miss Parkyn Hello, Jean.
Jean Gisele! (*She notes Miss Parkyn's state of dress*) Oh, I see! I assume the Minister did not go to the decency congress after all.
Miss Parkyn Right! We were working late, when I was taken suddenly ill, so he had to undress me to give me the kiss of life.
Jean Am I seriously expected to believe that?
Miss Parkyn (*cheerfully*) Of course not—any more than I believe you've grown a moustache. Very kinky!

Jean hastily detaches the moustache

(*Feeling Jean's dress*) I say, you're soaking.
Jean (*tearfully*) I got caught in that storm, without a coat.
Miss Parkyn (*soothingly*) Well, come on upstairs and take your dress off.
Jean I've got nothing else to put on.
Miss Parkyn (*giggling*) That doesn't matter! Nobody's wearing clothes this evening.

Act II

Miss Parkyn leads Jean off upstairs

The cupboard door opens and Potts emerges again. He is stunned by what he has seen and heard. It is better than his wildest dreams

Potts It's strip-off night! A foursome! (*He rubs his hands together*) I've got him! I've got him!

In the bedroom, Wendy makes herself pretty in front of the mirror. Potts darts back again as he hears someone coming

> *Barry enters from the kitchen munching a sandwich with a sausage in it. He crosses the living-room and enters the bedroom. Wendy turns with a welcoming smile. Barry stares, horrified. He closes the door, waving the sandwich*

Wendy Hello, darling!
Barry No! Enough's enough. Get dressed and get out of here!
Wendy (*incoherently*) Who—who are you, what are you doing?
Barry Yes. I recognize you. One of those girls who kidnapped me, aren't you? Well, get back to your pestiferous party. Get back and seduce someone else.
Wendy I—I don't know what you mean. I never seduced you in my life —did I?
Barry Out of my room! Go on, out! Out, out, out!
Wendy But it isn't your room. It's—this is Sir William Mainwaring-Brown's flat.
Barry Have you come to see *him*?
Wendy Yes—I have.
Barry (*shocked to the core*) Another! Great Scott!
Wendy Is he here?
Barry I'm not altogether sure. Who are you? What do you want with him?
Wendy He phoned me last night and asked me to come round. I said I couldn't make it—but now I can, and he'll be so pleased. Just to tell him Wendy is here.
Barry Wendy—yes, all right. (*He suddenly gives the biggest reaction of all. He gasps and points*) Wendy! That's how I know you! You're Mrs Thoroughgood, wife of that gossip columnist.
Wendy (*agonized*) Ssssh! Please! If my husband found out he'd ruin Billy. The paper's got a terrific circulation.
Barry So has the Minister, it seems. And he's not even been drugged! (*Going to the bedroom door*) Stay here and, if you don't want trouble— keep quiet.

Wendy sits on the bed, takes off her boots, and sprawls voluptuously. Barry hurries into the sitting-room, closing the door after him. As he passes the cupboard door a hand reaches out and grabs him, scaring him. Potts emerges, triumphant, carrying the bottle of champagne

Potts Why, it's you, Sergeant! It's me. I remembered. What you forgot. Why I'm here. Mainwaring-Brown. Heard rumours of goings-on. By Jingo! They were right. The place is fallen with crawling women. We've got him, Sarge. He's a dead duck, and so's the Government. (*He puts his finger to his nose and starts to withdraw into the cupboard*) But I'm not going to pounce till I catch him actually at it. (*Putting his finger to his lips*) Not a word. Not a word. (*He withdraws into the cupboard, closing the door*)

The Minister enters from the study

Minister Ah, I wanted to see you about why Miss Parkyn was . . .
Barry And I've got to see you. (*He carries out a series of inexplicable—to the Minister—pieces of mime designed to give away Potts's presence in the cupboard. In a hoarse whisper*) Danger lurks. Skeleton in the cupboard. Old Skeleton. (*He gives a fine mime performance of a doddering old man*) Not a word. Not a word.
Minister (*loudly*) What are you raving about?
Barry (*drawing nearer*) You're in *Potts* of trouble. (*Hissing*) You didn't know Snoopy was here . . .
Minister Of course I knew he was here. Him and his gladstone bag. Now about Miss Parkyn being in bed . . .
Barry (*agonized*) No! No! Worse is to come. There's another, in there. One of your mistr . . .

Miss Parkyn suddenly appears and comes downstairs

(*Seeing her, and promptly going into song*)
                   Mistress regrets she's unable
                   To sleep today-ay—Minister!
Minister Are you drunk?
Barry No! No! No!

Miss Parkyn moves to the bedroom door. Barry utters a strangled cry and cuts her off, placing himself against it, arms wide

You can't go in there!
Miss Parkyn Why not? I left my compact . . .
Barry No, they shall not pass.
Miss Parkyn I'm not going to stay there.
Barry No! No, no, no, no. (*He drives Miss Parkyn back across the room, below the Minister, then returns to the latter*)
                   Wendy-wippowill calls
                   And you'll get a fright—
                   Hot cha-cha-cha.
Minister He's gone!
Barry No! I just feel like singing. Do you know this one? (*Singing again*)
                   Wendy moon comes over the mountain,
                   Miss Parkyn will blow her top. Her top.

Act II

Minister I think the expression is don't call us, we'll call you.
Miss Parkyn I don't know about *me* blowing my top, but Jean will certainly blow hers if she finds you in this state.
Barry (*freezing*) J-Jean . . . Has she?
Miss Parkyn She's upstairs. Be down any moment. (*Indicating the bedroom*) If she isn't there already by way of the back stairs.
Barry Aaaagh! (*He charges into the bedroom, slamming the door behind him*)
Wendy What . . . ?
Barry Sssh!

Barry rushes past Wendy and goes out up the bedroom stairs

Minister Jean back here? This is awful.

Jean enters down the main stairs. She wears a rather fluffy robe over underwear. Her hair is loose

Jean Where's Barry?
Minister Looking for you.

Barry rushes downstairs to the bedroom

Barry (*to Wendy*) Keep quiet! (*He opens the bedroom door, colliding with Jean on the living-room side as he closes it*) Aaaagh! You're back. (*Humming loudly, he waltzes Jean up to the desk chair, then grabs the Minister and tangos him away. He sings*)
                Wendy—is done—
                And Government falls . . .
Minister He's off again!
Barry (*singing*) And so will you . . .

The Minister pushes him off violently

Minister What the hell is this "When daylight falls, When day is done—Wenday . . . " (*He gets it*) Wendy! *Wendy!*

The Minister freezes, looks sick, glances at the bedroom door, then at Barry. Barry nods

Barry Yes, Wenday I had a *Thoroughgood* song in my heart and that's the *nearly* naked truth.

The Minister controls himself with a visible effort. He turns to Jean and Miss Parkyn

Minister Would you ladies kindly leave us? Barry needs urgent psychiatric help.
Miss Parkyn Going to lay *him* on your couch now?
Minister Get out!

Jean and Miss Parkyn exit to the hall

Wendy Thoroughgood here? I mean in there?
Barry Yes, and stripped for action. How *could* you?
Minister There's a perfectly simple explanation. She's a lady dedicated to charity work. We are rehearsing a play.
Barry (*bitterly*) A passion play? And what charity? The Relief of Tired Ministers?
Minister No. The Avoid the Children Fund. (*He goes to the bedroom door*) I'm going to talk to her. Keep cave, and if anyone comes—(*putting a biscuit from the bowl into Barry's mouth*)—bark.
Barry Bark?

The Minister goes into the bedroom. Wendy grabs him and pulls his face right into her cleavage

Minister Wendy, darling.
Wendy Billy-willy. Harold had to leave London suddenly on a story, so I'm here after all.
Minister You should have warned me.
Wendy I wanted to surprise you.
Minister You've certainly done that. But you'll have to leave, Wendy. I'm a sick man. The verdict came through tonight.
Wendy You're not going to die?
Minister The doctor says if I put my feet up and get straight to bed, alone, I *may* pull through tonight.
Wendy (*releasing him for the first time; suspiciously*) Billy-willy, I heard voices.
Minister You are another Joan of Arc! I always said so.
Wendy Women's voices.
Minister Ah! Yes, that's a very tragic story.
Wendy What is?
Minister (*clearly stumped*) You may well ask, would you excuse me just one moment, thank you very much. (*He goes into the sitting-room, closing the bedroom door, and taps Barry on the shoulder, startling him*)
Barry Woof, woof, woof.
Minister Shut up! How do I get her out of there across the sitting-room and out of the flat?
Barry What have you done to her? Can't she walk?
Minister Without Jean or Parkyn seeing her, you fool! They might barge in any moment, and with my luck they probably will.
Barry (*brightly*) I know.

During Barry's subsequent display the Minister watches him with slow, burning contempt and fury

You pretend you're a bullfighter.
Minister A bullfighter?
Barry Yes. You hold a policeman's cape in front of you, suspended on a golf-club, making passes and saying "Olé" and things like that, and

Act II

the girl hides behind the cape and you sweep her across the room and out of the door saying "Hey toro!" and "Viva Zapata!" (*He catches the Minister's grim look*) I know it sounds silly, but . . .
Minister Then why make the bloody suggestion in the first place?
Barry But it works. I tell you, I . . .
Minister I am *not* a bullfighter. I'm not going to pretend to be a bullfighter. I'm a Minister of State—until tomorrow, if I don't get out of this.
Barry I know. (*He suddenly waves his sandwich*) I know! You put her in a sandwich.
Minister (*grabbing Barry by the lapels*) One more idiotic . . .
Barry No! I saw it in a show. This sausage is the girl, and you and I are the pieces of bread. You stand her between us, squash right up, and the one in front always faces whoever comes into the room, so they can't see the girl in the middle.
Minister Do you know something? That might just work. Does Wendy know who you are?
Barry (*miserably*) I don't think so. I'm beginning to wonder myself.
Minister (*patting his shoulder*) Cheer up. See me safely through this and, who knows, one day you may be Deputy Prime Minister. Come with me. I need your help.

The Minister leads Barry back into the bedroom

Ah, Wendy. I believe you've already met Bishop Ovis, haven't you?

Barry gives a start

Poor Barry's reverend twin brother.
Wendy Bishop! He isn't dressed like a bishop.
Minister Even bishops have to get into mufti after—er—taking a bath.
Wendy But why is a bishop taking a bath here?
Minister (*nervily*) Because he was *filthy*. (*To Barry*) Isn't that right?
Barry Yes. I fell down and dirtied my canonicals.
Wendy But why here?
Minister That's the tragic story I was telling you. He flew in this morning to effect a reconciliation between the Church of Australia and the Church of England.
Wendy I didn't know they'd quarrelled.
Minister Bitterly, and that's the point. The press have got on to it, and half Fleet Street will be here any moment for a press conference.
Wendy (*in horror*) Oh, no!
Minister You can imagine what they'll say if they find *you* here, dressed like that.
Wendy (*in panic*) Oh, my goodness!
Minister You know their filthy minds. You are married to one of them.
Wendy (*flapping about*) What am I going to do?

The Minister picks up Wendy's clothes and gives them to her in a bundle

Minister Ovis is going to show us how to get you out of here. (*To Barry*) How does it work? And it better.
Barry Stand her between us, and if anyone comes in we must be sure to face them. The secret is military precision, so squash right up.

The Minister and Barry sandwich Wendy between them, all three standing as close together as possible, with Wendy virtually squashed and suffocated. Barry takes the front, the Minister bringing up the rear

Now? By the front quick march! Left, right, left, right.

As they get to the communicating door they mark time, back up as Barry opens it, then all three march out to the sitting-room, squashed close together, their three visible legs marching in time. The Minister's and Barry's shoulders are forced backward and forward so as to conceal as much of Wendy as possible from the sideways view

As the three get level with the cupboard, Jean suddenly enters from the hall

Halt!

The three halt, standing like ramrods, facing Jean

Jean goes there!
Jean Now what are you playing at?

Jean starts to circle them, and they sway round to keep Barry facing her

Barry Practice. The march past for the Queen's birthday.
Jean The Members of Parliament don't march past on the Queen's birthday.
Barry One of Ted's new ideas. (NOTE: *The Christian name of the current Prime Minister is substituted here*) Front Benchers at the back. Back Benchers at the front.

Jean smells chicanery and starts to move back again

Alley-oop! Left, right, left, right, left, right.

The three perform an agile hoppity-skippity jump in perfect unison so that Jean still only faces Barry at the head of the line. Jean moves forward towards Barry

To the rear—double! Left, right, left, right.
Miss Parkyn (*off*) Jean . . .
Barry Parkyn ahoy! Left wheel——

As Miss Parkyn threatens to come on the Minister doubles from the rear of the line up stage to above Wendy, who doubles backwards a pace, and they all double back until Wendy is hidden from Miss Parkyn by the cupboard and the Minister doubles to between Wendy and Barry, who is still facing Jean

Act II

Miss Parkyn enters from the hall and comes to Jean

—left, right, left, right.
Miss Parkyn I wondered . . . (*She reacts*) What goes on?
Jean You tell me!
Barry Return to base. Left, right, left, right, left, right.

They all three trot back into the bedroom. Unhappily, though, Wendy drops her hot pants below the cupboard

Lep! Ri! Lep! Ri! Lep! God Save the Queen! Halt. Fall out. (*Finding himself inches from Wendy's bosom*) No! Don't!
Minister You can forget all about being Deputy P.M. Berk!

Simultaneously, two things happen: Wendy discovers the loss of her clothes, Jean discovers the clothes on the sitting-room floor

Jean Hot pants!
Wendy My hot pants!
Miss Parkyn (*grabbing the hot pants and storming into the bedroom*) Hot pants.

Jean follows Miss Parkyn into the bedroom

Minister (*taking the garment*) Ah, my hot pants.
Miss Parkyn And who have we here, Superman?
Minister These are—this is one of Mr Ovis's constituents, the widow Blenkinsop.
Wendy (*with a cry*) It's your Parkyn creature! (*She drives the Minister round the bed and hits him with her bag*)

Miss Parkyn follows and Wendy turns on her

I knew you were after her!
Miss Parkyn Don't you creature me, you—constituent.
Wendy (*indicating Jean*) And that other one! Two of them! You disgusting brute. So that's why you wanted to get rid of me.

Wendy clouts the Minister hard. He doubles up, completely winded, and collapses, gasping and groaning, on the bed. Wendy wades into Miss Parkyn. Jean goes to the foot of the bed and lies across, trying to part them. Barry also moves forward to try to intervene. They all fall on the bed, fighting noisily to join the Minister

The window curtains part suddenly and Ruff enters

Ruff My Gawd! It's another bleeding orgy!

The fighting stops. All look at Ruff except the Minister, who is still incapacitated. Barry gets off the bed and goes to Ruff. Miss Parkyn, Wendy and Jean also rise

And what's the meaning of this?

Barry (*with a French accent*) Er, er, er, er, I'm Cecil Ovis from Australia and this is my wife Mon . . .
Ruff I know who you say you are, sir. I asked what you were at.
Barry (*with a German accent*) Oh—ve vere playing und game.
Ruff What game?
Barry (*with a West Country accent*) Um—zardines. You know zardines.
Ruff I've eaten them, sir, and as a child I've played the game of that name —but never without my clothes on.
Barry It's strip sardines. An Australian game. (*With his Australian accent*) It's whacko-bluey.
Ruff Bluey, certainly. Seen nothing like it since I raided a cinema club last Saturday.
Barry Well, it is nice to see you again, Sergeant . . .
Ruff Inspector.
Barry Inspector. I didn't catch your name?
Ruff Ruff, sir—and I can be. Very.
Barry Inspector Ruff, that's it. So now you know everybody.
Ruff No, sir. Everybody knows me but—(*looking at Wendy and Jean*)— I don't think I've had the—(*he frowns and peers at Jean*)—wait a minute, though, I know you, don't I?
Barry (*urgently*) No! You've never met her! You couldn't have. Either of them.

Ruff brings out his notebook and pencil, opens it and waits expectantly. The Minister has now recovered sufficiently to sit up and take notice

Ruff Don't tell me! Not more visitors from the outback?
Barry (*relieved*) That's it! Meet my cousin Glenda Spring and her cousin —Spring—er . . .
Minister Be quiet! (*He sits up with Wendy's handbag over his arm*) It's time to tell the Inspector the truth.
Barry (*shocked*) Oh, is it? Oh dear! Oh, well!

Barry is obviously shattered by this, and the three girls also look unpleasantly surprised. Only Ruff looks pleased, and keeps his pencil poised

Ruff I thought you'd get round to it sooner or later, Sir William.
Minister It's useless trying to pull the wool over your eyes any longer. The real truth, Inspector, is that Monica Ovis—(*indicating Miss Parkyn*) —that is, Cecil's wife . . .
Ruff Yes, sir, I think I have the relationship almost straighter than you— but carry on.
Minister Monica Ovis is gravely ill.

All look surprised at this. Barry in particular looks hopeful again. Miss Parkyn collapses prettily on Barry's shoulder

Miss Parkyn (*dramatically*) Oh!
Ruff Really, sir?
Minister Yes, really. Isn't that so, Cecil?
Barry Oh, yes. Too right. Dreadfully right.

Act II

Ruff You'd never think so.
Barry That's the tragedy. Blooming one moment, gathered the next.
Ruff Are you seriously saying your wife is *in extremis*?
Barry Extremely.
Minister As a matter of fact, when you burst in that first time, her husband and myself were actually giving her the kiss of life.
Ruff *Both* at the same time?
Barry Yes.
Ruff She's only got one mouth.
Barry (*stumped*) In extreme cases . . .
Minister (*hastily*) Cecil! Her husband and I were taking it in turns in a desperate endeavour to keep her going.
Ruff Well, I never! And what is her trouble, if I may ask?
Minister By a strange coincidence, *her* hot-water bottle had leaked, too.

Ruff raises his eyes skywards and sighs

We had an electric blanket in the bed . . .
Ruff Don't bother to go on, Sir William.
Minister I insist on going on. You asked. On getting into bed, Mrs Ovis received a severe electric shock resulting in ventricular fibrillation.
Ruff Vent . . . eh?
Minister Ventricular fibrillation. (*He puts his hand in his pocket and surreptitiously consults a piece of paper concealed in his palm*) In layman's terms, she has a serious condition of both ventricles.
Ruff I didn't think ladies had ventricles.
Barry Yes! Those are her chambers.
Ruff Beg your pardon, sir?
Barry (*indicating*) Heart chambers.
Minister Resulting in fibrillation, loss of breath and complete paralysis of both lungs.
Ruff (*who doesn't believe a word; moving towards Barry*) Very nasty, very nasty. (*To Barry, suddenly*) You should have sent for a doctor.
Barry I did, I did. (*Having a brilliant idea*) And *she* came! (*He indicates Jean*) An expert on Venter Fib, it, them, meet Dr Schutz.

The Minister throws up his hands with a growl of despair. Unfortunately, Wendy stands between Barry and Jean and takes this to be her cue to start acting. As Jean starts to move, Wendy walks towards Ruff with outstretched hand

Wendy How do you do. I am Doctor Schloss.
Ruff Schloss?
Wendy Schkoll.
Jean Schwartz.
Miss Parkyn Schmertz.
Barry Schutz.
Minister Shut up!
Ruff You sent for this doctor, sir?
Barry I wouldn't send for anybody else.

Ruff Understandable, sir. I can see her credentials are outstanding.
Barry Well now, if you don't mind, Inspector, my wife is due for another quick kiss of life, so if you haven't any more questions . . .
Ruff But I have, sir.
Barry Oh. That's a pity
Ruff (*indicating Jean*) You still haven't introduced me to this other lady who I never met before.
Barry How stupid of me! This is Nurse Witherspoon. She is assistant to Dr Schni-schner—er—schn . . . Nurse Woodenwithers. Inspector—er . . .
Ruff Ruff. Delighted to meet you again, Nurse. Yes, well, let's have a little recap, shall we? As at this time we have a—(*consulting his notebook*) —Mr and Mrs Cecil Ovis from Gladys Springs down under; Mrs Ovis being under the weather with Virginal Tribulations . . .
Barry Oh, no! No, no, no, no. (*He forgets it himself*) Ventriloquist fib . . .
Miss Parkyn Ventricular fibrillation.
Ruff Thank you, ma'am. And called in to give medical assistance is Dr Schloss, Schkoll, Schwartz, Schmertz, Schutz, Schultz or Shut-up, depending on who's speaking, accompanied—(*moving to Jean then back to Barry*)—by Nurse Witherspoon or Woodenwithers, who bears an uncanny resemblance to Mr Barry Ovis's fiancée who I met earlier this evening.
Barry (*desperation stakes*) They're first cousins, twice removed.

Miss Parkyn suppresses a delighted giggle

Ruff Dear me! I think she's fibrillating.
Miss Parkyn (*controlling herself*) I'll be fine.
Barry If she isn't, on your head be it.
Ruff Yes, sir. (*He comes face to face with Wendy's bosom and is riveted*) This may seem a stupid question, Doctor, but do you usually make your outside calls dressed in underwear and nighties?
Wendy Oh, yes!
Barry Oh, yes! She's a night doctor and she's a night nurse, so, when they're staying the night, they take their nighties.
Wendy That's right!
Barry And anyway, you can't do it properly in your clothes.
Ruff Do *what*?
Barry Artificial insemi . . . respiration. Have *you* ever tried giving the kiss of life with your clothes on?
Ruff No, sir, and I don't intend trying it with them off, either. (*He closes his notebook with a snap*) Full marks for trying, gents, but it simply won't wash.
Minister Are you calling us liars?
Ruff Let me put it this way, Sir William. If I was your wife I wouldn't have a pencil in my hand right now, I'd have a rolling-pin.
Minister (*rising*) I prefer to leave my wife out of this.
Ruff (*with a rare smile*) I don't blame you.
Barry You may care to know that Dr Schmaltz is Lady Mainwaring-

Act II   51

Brown's personal physician and Nurse Woodenspoon has sat by her bedside on countless occasions . . .

Ruff (*cutting in*) Yes, Minister. Well, that's easily checked, isn't it? (*He puts his notebook away and walks into the sitting-room*)

All follow him in this order: Minister, Barry, Miss Parkyn, Jean, Wendy

Minister Oh, no, just a minute, please, excuse me!
Ruff Meanwhile——

He stops abruptly below the main door to the hall and turns, which makes the Minister stop dead and the rest all pile up against the one in front, going "ooh!" as they do so

——it's only fair to warn you that anyone leaving here will be followed—for their protection, of course. Good night, Sir William.

Ruff exits to the hall

Minister (*until Ruff has gone*) Good night. Do call again some year.

The front door bangs. The Minister turns on Barry like a tiger

Nurse Witherspoon! He'd already met Jean, you raving nincompoop!
Barry We're done for anyway. What with him and—(*he indicates the cupboard*)—and . . .
Minister Shut up! One thing may save us. If Sexgon Blake comes back, Cecil and Monica Ovis will have disappeared and Barry Ovis will be back safe and sound, recovering from a quick bout of amnesia.
Miss Parkyn No good.
Minister Eh?
Miss Parkyn He'd only have to check with the police outside, who'd say they didn't see anyone leaving or Mr Ovis returning.
Minister A good point, which I may well raise in the House as an example of growing police inefficiency.
Miss Parkyn You'd be on safer ground offering him a whopping great bribe.
Minister Not a chance. I know the type—vilely incorruptible.
Miss Parkyn All right, so Mr Ovis miraculously returns. Now what are you going to do with me?
Minister If and when the detective comes back you'll have to hide. Meanwhile pop into the study and start drafting a statement for the press on Barry Ovis's disappearance, will you? Keep it short—overwork leading to temporary amnesia.
Miss Parkyn (*shaking her head*) And the best of British luck.

Miss Parkyn exits to the study

Minister (*to Barry*) Now—oh damn! Moustache!
Jean I bought a false one. It's upstairs somewhere.
Minister Clever girl! Go and get it.

Jean exits upstairs

(*To Barry*) Do something about your appearance, for heaven's sake.
Wendy Now perhaps you'll tell me what that Parkyn creature is doing here?

Barry turns and listens with a disillusioned, disapproving expression

Minister Wendy, darling, it's a very tragic story. I certainly don't want to hear it again. Look, why don't you go upstairs and wait for me, eh?
Wendy Oh, no, the bishop wouldn't like it.
Minister The bishop isn't going to get it.

Wendy exits upstairs

The Minister turns and sees Barry staring at him

What are you staring at?
Barry You.
Minister Take that disapproving look off your face, for a start.
Barry I can't. I'm shattered at your behaviour. I tried to warn you, but now it's too late and you deserve all you're going to get.
Minister Are you threatening me, Ovis?
Barry *I'm* not, but look in that cupboard and do your explaining to him. He's seen and heard everything.
Minister What are you talking about? Who?

Barry walks to the cupboard door and opens it

Barry All right, you'd better cóme out now, Mr Potts.

We may expect to see Potts standing, triumphant, inside the cupboard; but this is not the case. He is seated on the box, leaning against the wall, fast asleep, with the empty champagne bottle clasped in his arms. The Minister's breath comes in a shocked hiss

Minister Snoopy! Why the hell didn't you tell me . . . ?
Barry I *tried* half a dozen times.
Minister Is he dead, I hope?
Barry (*examining Potts*) No, asleep.
Minister How much does he know? How much did he hear?
Barry (*shrugging*) He knows you've filled the place with women.
Minister Pity we can't have him put down. He'd be grateful. He's ga-ga half the time. Look, if we can straighten this thing up before he wakes, *then* we'll say he dreamt the whole thing. Sh, sh! He's waking.
Potts (*in his sleep*) Thank you, Enid, dear. Now tuck me in, will you?
Minister Tuck him in, tuck him in.

Barry tucks Potts in

Potts That's a good girl. Now give Grandad a kiss. Come on, Enid, give Grandad a good night kiss.

Act II

Minister Go on, Enid! Give Grandad a good night kiss.
Barry I don't kiss men!
Minister He's not a man. He's a monster. Kiss him!

Barry submits and kisses Potts on the forehead

Potts (*contented*) You're a good girl, even if you didn't shave this morning.

The Minister carefully closes the cupboard door

> *Damina steps through the bedroom window into the room. She tiptoes to the communicating door and listens*

Minister If you're putting on a false moustache you'd better get some proper clothes on.
Barry I haven't any proper clothes. All my stuff's in my flat.
Minister You didn't walk back here naked, did you?
Barry Of course I didn't. But I was in a very way-out outfit. You see, they whipped my suit at that party.
Minister Some party! You must have something you can put on, surely?
Barry There's only my wedding outfit . . . .
Minister That'll be fine. Now, here is your story. You got dressed, went out for a walk, and lost your memory. (*He adopts a friendly, conspiratorial air*) We're in this together, chum, you and I . . .
Barry Oh, no, we're not! I may have made an idiot of myself, but at least I was kidnapped and drugged. But you—you can damn well stew in your own juice.
Minister (*with a martyred air*) Well, there's loyalty for you!
Barry Loy . . . you dare talk about loyalty! You bring *two* girls here on the same night to one flat on *one* night for—immoral purposes. I'm not even married, yet I'd die rather than bring one. The mind boggles.
Minister Oh, boggle off!

As Barry goes haughtily into the bedroom, Damina steps quickly behind the door and then hides behind the bedroom cupboard. The Minister helps himself to some caviar. Barry slams the door and does not see Damina as he walks to the cupboard, removes his dressing-gown and takes off his pyjama bottoms. He leaves the white top on and reaches into the cupboard to take out the grey wedding trousers

Damina Coooeee!
Barry (*whirling round*) Oh, no!

Damina runs forward and places a hand over Barry's mouth. The Minister decides to have another go at Barry and enters the bedroom. He stops in his tracks as he sees Barry trouserless, with Damina

Minister Well! Well! Who's boggling now?
Barry (*in a cracked voice*) Not me! She just—walked in.
Minister You know this girl?
Barry Well, on and off—I mean, once. We . . .

Damina I didn't come to see him. I came to see you.
Minister (*closing the door*) Me? I don't know you—(*unsure*)—do I?
Damina Not yet. I got a proposition for you from Johnny Solnik.
Minister (*blankly*) Johnny Solnik?
Barry (*in a big reaction*) Johnny *Solnik*!
Minister Who the hell is Johnny Solnik?
Barry He's that agitator who's always agitating about everything.
Minister That anarchist? (*To Damina*) Sorry, I don't accept propositions from people like that. (*To Barry*) Nice company you keep, Ovis.
Damina Don't you be beastly to him. *You* can't talk.
Minister (*with hauteur*) I beg your pardon?
Damina Remember when you hid under the bed—(*she gestures with her forefingers and thumb*)—and whispered "tweak-tweak"?
Minister (*thunderstruck*) How do you know about that?
Damina It was *me* you tweak-tweaked. Have I made my point?
Minister Couple of points, I'd say. What is this proposition?
Damina Johnny and lots of others think you're being undemocratic. You keep attacking freedom of speech and the right of protest and say you're going to bring in laws to prevent it . . .
Minister To prevent anarchy. You're damn right we are.
Damina Well, we don't think you should.
Minister Ha! And how do you propose to stop us?
Damina By circulating the pictures all over London.
Minister What pictures?
Damina The ones I took through that window tonight. You and Barry in bed with a bird, then larking about in a bed with three birds . . .
Minister (*to Barry*) If the Government falls you are responsible. *You.*
Barry Me?
Minister You! You brought her here.
Barry I know I did, but . . . (*He turns to Damina*) I don't know how you can do this. You said I was off the hook.
Minister She's only bluffing, anyway. If she'd been taking photographs at that window we'd have seen the flash.

Damina unzips her jacket to its fullest extent. She pulls out the object on the chain round her neck

Damina Minox camera. Super-fast film. There's no need for flash . . .

The Minister lunges for the camera. They struggle. Damina gets a hand free and pulls up her jacket zip. The Minister's head is bent towards her chest. The resulting action causes the Minister's dressing-gown to get caught in her zip. The Minister is therefore welded to her with his head on her chest.
NOTE: *The scene is played without actual zipping, the actors keeping close together*

No, you don't . . .

Barry meanwhile has started to put on his wedding trousers

Minister Ovis! She's got me caught in her zip. Get the camera.

Act II

Damina No.

Barry, half pulling on his trousers, runs awkwardly to join them. He starts to put his braces over his shoulders

Minister Come on! Get the camera.

Barry puts both arms round Damina from behind, and his trousers promptly fall down. He pulls them up, operates the zip, and inadvertently zips himself to the back of Damina's jacket

Well, what's holding you up?

Barry She is. (*He tries to move back*) I'm zipped too.

The Minister snarls

Damina Now keep your cool, Minnie. Take off the dressing-gown.

Minister What? And add indecent exposure to my crimes? No fear! You take this thing off. Pull it over your head. Go on.

Damina tries to pull her jacket over her head, but this causes a very painful tugging at Barry's trouser zipper. He leaps up on tiptoe and gives a high-pitched cry

Barry Ow! Stop that!

Damina All right! All right! Don't get all uptight.

Barry That's the trouble. It's right up tight.

Damina This isn't going to work unless I pull *him* over my head too.

Minister Pull him over your head, then. Go on.

Barry (*shrilly*) No.

Minister Oh, let's go into the other room.

They start a painful, combined movement through the bedroom door. It is the sandwich route again, but without rhythm and in slow motion. The Minister walks blindly backwards with his head still resting on Damina's chest and his behind stuck out. Barry moves in a series of frog-like jumps, giving little squeaks of pain with each jump

Barry Wait! I've just had a flash of inspiration.

Minister Well, don't flash it here.

Barry If I can get my hands inside my trousers, perhaps I can burst open the zip from inside.

Minister Stop gassing and get on with it.

Barry Yes, all right, it's rather a tight fit. Wait a minute. There we are. Right. Are you ready? (*He jerks*) Ayar, ayar, ayar. It's no good, it doesn't work. As you were.

Minister Come on!

They continue the move into the sitting-room until they are below the archway. Suddenly the Minister gives a yell

Oh! My slipped disc! I've got to sit down. I've got to sit down.

Barry manoeuvres round and sits in the swivel desk chair with the others leaning on him

I've got to sit down, you nit, not you.

Barry rises and they all twist until the Minister sits, going "Ah!" with relief

Barry Ooh!
Minister Ah!
Barry Ooh!
Minister Ah!
Barry Ah!
Minister Ooh!
Barry Ah!
Minister Ooh! Right, Ovis, get the scissors.
Barry (*alarmed*) Scissors! What for?
Minister To cut out your zip, of course.
Barry You can't do that!
Minister *I* can't, but you can. Then you can get married and live happily ever after—if you're very careful.
Barry Yes, but what will Moss Bros say?
Minister (*enraged*) The fate of the Government hangs on this, and you worry about the brothers Moss! Get on with it.

Barry tries to free his hands

Barry I can't, anyway. My hands are stuck in my trousers.
Minister (*laughing*) One day, of course, we shall be free of all this, and we'll be strolling through the park on a beautiful summer's day on our way to the House—and I'll *kill* you! (*He angrily seizes the scissors from the desk and brandishes them*) Right, *I'll* have a stab at it.

Barry reacts in dismay. The Minister starts to push the scissors round the outside of Damina then in again towards Barry's zip

Now, if I can circumscribe ...
Barry *No!!*
Minister Circum*scribe!* Go around the side, you fool. (*He tries to get the scissors round the outside but cannot make it. He grunts with the exertion*) That's no good. I can't do it from this angle. Miss——

The Minister returns to the original position and addresses Damina, who is quietly enjoying all this

—legs astride, please.

Damina puts her legs astride. The Minister gets his arm through them with the scissors. He cannot see what he is doing, since his face is still clamped to Damina's chest

Now keep very still. Remember I'm flying blind.
Barry Please! Be dreadfully careful.

The Minister moves the scissors forward. He makes contact. Barry yells

Higher! Lower! To the right! No! *Your* right. Oooh! That was a near thing!

The buzzer on the house telephone suddenly lets out a loud and startling buzz. The Minister gives a jump. Barry yells with pain

Aaaaaaagh! You've done it—I'm ruined.

They all move in ungainly fashion so that the Minister can reach the house telephone with his free hand. He answers it

Minister Yes?... No! I don't want to ... He is? Damn! (*He hangs up*) That was the hall porter. That ruddy detective is on his way up. So now we must go for broke.
Barry (*groaning*) Nothing to win and all to lose!
Minister Shut up! Open up!

Damina stands astride. The Minister goes to work through her legs with the scissors. Barry writhes, moans, and tries to keep still. The Minister cuts Barry free and then frees himself. Barry now has a gaping hole in the front of his trousers. His trapped hands show in the hole

Now listen, young woman, if this detective finds you here we're sunk, but *so are you*. You get a long stretch for blackmail. Come with me. (*He takes her into the bedroom*) Now then, hide under that bed until we get rid of the detective and then *perhaps* we can talk turkey.

Barry moves to the Minister with his trousers gaping wide and his hands still inside them and visible near his crutch

Not a pretty sight.
Damina Look, why am I always under the bed? (*She gets under*)
Minister You play your cards right and you can work your way up. (*He turns to Barry, sees the gaping fly*) When's milking time? Do something about that, for heaven's sake.
Barry I *told* you. I haven't any other clothes.
Minister Well then, turn those trousers back to front and keep facing him. Where *is* Jean with your moustache? He's *got* to see you as Barry Ovis.

Miss Parkyn enters from the study and heads towards the bedroom

The front doorbell rings

Quick, oh dear. (*He opens the communicating door and sees Miss Parkyn*) That's the detective. Monica Ovis is supposed to have disappeared. Under the bed.

Miss Parkyn runs to the bed and starts to get under

Miss Parkyn There's a bird here ...
Minister Not my pigeon.

The doorbell rings again

Wendy enters downstairs

Wendy Billy!

The Minister takes Wendy and thrusts her into the bedroom cupboard, where Barry is selecting a tie

Minister If you love your country, Wendy, into that cupboard and stay quiet.

The doorbell rings again and goes on ringing

Wendy I do love my country, but . . .

The Minister shuts the cupboard door. The doorbell rings again, long and hard

   The Minister crosses the sitting-room and exits to the hall

Wendy reappears in the cupboard

Wendy I don't understand. I'm the doctor. I shouldn't be hiding.
Barry He's lost his head.
Wendy (*coming out*) Then shouldn't I stay outside?
Barry No. Do what he says. He's used to lying. That's why he's a senior minister.

   Barry pushes Wendy back, then takes his jacket and ascot and exits up the bedroom stairs.
   The Minister and Ruff enter from the hall. Ruff carries a file. They come below the cupboard

Ruff You were a long time answering the door, sir.
Minister Yes, I didn't hear you the first three times.

Ruff opens the file, takes out some photographs and shows one to the Minister

Ruff What would you say that photograph was, Sir William?

The Minister pushes Ruff's arm away to its fullest extent and then backs to the desk, squinting hard

Minister That's a chap dancing with two constables.
Ruff He's coshing them, actually.
Minister Is he? Oh, I see.
Ruff It's that hippy who escaped into this building. Taken by an amateur photographer who happened to be standing near by.
Minister Quite a day for the photographers.
Ruff Do you notice a startling resemblance between this hippy and your old friend Cecil Ovis?

   Jean enters downstairs carrying the moustache. She does not immediately see Ruff

Jean Sorry about the moustache, Sir William . . .

Act II

Minister So am I, Nurse, but never mind. Men often make passes at girls with moustaches. (*Leading her back towards the stairs*) Some men even *prefer* hairy women. (*Sotto voce*) Go the other way. Hurry!

Jean nods and exits upstairs

(*Returning to Ruff*) Funny creatures, aren't they?

Ruff Aren't they, sir. But for the moment let's stick with your *old friend* Cecil Ovis, shall we?

Minister I didn't say he was my old friend. That's what he said. He told me he was Barry's brother, and who was I to doubt him?

Ruff You just accepted an impostor, without question, as brother of the missing man?

Minister Does it matter? Barry Ovis isn't missing any more. He has returned safe and sound.

Ruff (*astonished*) What!

Minister A day of complete amnesia, but he'll be fine.

Ruff Oh, I see, and what did *he* say when he met his brother who wasn't?

Minister Ah—er, well, they never actually met, because the couple calling themselves Cecil and Monica Ovis have gone.

Ruff (*thundering*) Gone!

Minister (*improvising hard*) Gone, yes. I thought it was strange because when I told him that Barry was back Cecil merely said "Whacko!" and scarpered. (*Overacting surprise like mad*) Oooh! You were right all the time. He wasn't Barry's brother at all! Well done! Good lord! (*He pats Ruff's back*) Good work, Inspector.

Barry, wearing his trousers back to front and carrying the moustache, runs down the bedroom stairs, followed by Jean. He sticks the moustache on

Ruff You know, Sir William, as a liar you're beginning to disappoint me. However, the camera never lies. (*He gives the photo to the Minister*) That's upside down, Sir William.

In the bedroom Barry drops the moustache, which sticks to the carpet. Wendy opens the door of the cupboard and looks out

Wendy It's dreadfully hot in here. I think I'm going to faint. (*She screams*)
Ruff What's that?

Ruff opens the bedroom door. Wendy retreats and closes the cupboard door. Barry, his back to the door, scrabbles to get the moustache off the carpet. Ruff and the Minister enter the bedroom. The Minister sees only Barry's back. He looks relieved

Minister Ah, Barry! You haven't met Inspector Ruff, have you?

Barry straightens up and turns with a gasp

Ruff (*in a roar*) It's *him*! It's that hippy, sir. Watch it!

The Minister moves fast, shoving Ruff so that he sprawls by the bed. The Minister puts his foot on Ruff's back and pushes him down each time he tries to rise

Minister (*to Barry*) You swine! Impostor! (*He seizes Barry, puts his face near, and hisses*) Pretend to hit me and run.

Barry clouts the Minister and runs off up the bedroom stairs

Pretend, I said, you fool! (*He collapses near Ruff*)

Ruff rises and rushes after Barry, but the Minister grabs his leg as he goes, and hangs on

Ruff Will you let go, Sir William?
Minister Certainly. I beg your pardon.

Ruff exits up the bedroom stairs

Miss Parkyn's head emerges from under the bed

Miss Parkyn You're sunk. Try the bribe.

The Minister aims a symbolic kick at her

Minister Get back under! (*To Jean*) Where's that moustache?
Jean Here, stuck to the carpet.
Minister Don't stick it on the carpet, stick it on his lip.

The Minster goes into the sitting-room. Jean gets the moustache free and follows him

Barry rushes down the main stairs

Jean grabs Barry and pulls him back into the bedroom, slamming the door. The Minister goes towards the hall

Ruff, breathing stertorously, comes down the main stairs

The Minister gives a shout

That way!

The Minister rushes off to the hall. Ruff follows him

In the bedroom, Jean slaps the moustache on to Barry's upper lip. She helps him into his jacket, clips his tie round his neck and puts his top hat on his head

Barry How do I look?
Jean Lovely. Now go in and act.
Barry Act what?

Act II

Jean Yourself, you idiot! (*She turns to the window*)

Barry goes into the sitting-room, closing the bedroom door

> *Ruff runs in from the hall, followed by the Minister. The Minister looks greatly relieved to see Barry as himself*

Ruff I wish you'd stop helping me. It doesn't help.
Minister Ah! You haven't met Barry Ovis, have you? Ovis, Ruff, Ruff, Ovis. Ovis, Ruff.
Ruff (*nodding*) How do, sir.
Barry How do you do?
Ruff So you're back.
Barry Yes, I've been having a bout of amnesia.
Ruff Yes, do you have a brother, sir?
Barry I—I forget. I've still got a touch of it.
Ruff There is or was a man here posing as your brother, Cecil, about your build, clean-shaven, in shirt-sleeves. Have you seen him?
Barry Yes, a man did rush by. With the back of his trousers hanging out.
Ruff Which way did he go?
Barry I forget.
Ruff Oh, yes? (*He gives Barry an old-fashioned look and goes into the bedroom. To Jean*) Have you seen . . . ?
Jean That man? Yes, he appeared just there and ran back up when he saw me.

> *Ruff exits up the bedroom stairs*

Barry turns to the drinks table and pours himself a neat Scotch. He drains this at a gulp and gets a paroxysm of coughing. Choking, he turns round so that his back is briefly to the audience. The paroxysm subsides. He draws a deep breath, squares his shoulders, turns round—to reveal that, unknown to him, the moustache has come off again. NOTE: *He has in fact taken it off and stuck it on his hat. Jean comes from the bedroom*

Barry! Moustache!
Barry Here . . . (*He feels his lip*) Oh gosh! Where did it go?

The Minister, Barry and Jean all go down on their knees and start crawling about looking desperately for the moustache. Barry ends up between the others

> *Ruff comes noisily down the main stairs*

Barry sees Ruff and rises. As he rises, Jean grabs hold of his jacket. Barry runs out of it, throws his tie down, and goes into the bedroom

> *Barry exits up the bedroom stairs*

Jean opens the sideboard cupboard, throws the jacket and tie in, and closes the door. The Minister grabs Ruff by the arm as he runs by. Jean goes to the bedroom door and holds it open

Ruff Will you let go of my bleeding arm, sir?
Minister (*pushing Ruff hard so that he goes to the bedroom window*) So sorry!

Ruff turns, gives them both a filthy look, and runs up the bedroom stairs

Jean Moustache! We must find it.

The Minister looks on the floor in the bedroom. Miss Parkyn's head emerges from under the bed

Miss Parkyn Do the American air bases serve sausages in their canteens?
Minister (*with a snarl*) I'll call the President on Monday on the hot dog line.

The Minister joins Jean in the sitting-room, closing the door. Jean finds the moustache on the hat

Jean Got it!

Barry enters down the main stairs

Rather like passing the flag in a relay race, Jean passes him the moustache

Barry Thank you very much!

Barry runs through the bedroom door and exits up the stairs, trying to put on the moustache as he goes.
Ruff, visibly tiring, comes down the main stairs

Jean (*pointing to the study*) That way.
Ruff (*halting*) That way? Right. Then I'm going *this* way.

Ruff turns right round and heads back the way he came

Minister Damn! He plays poker.

Barry runs down the bedroom stairs, moustache clamped with one hand to his lip. He jumps down the steps, runs across the bedroom and enters the sitting-room

Barry The moustache, it won't stick—fluff on it—fluff on it.

Barry exits up the main stairs.
Ruff enters the bedroom, crosses, and comes into the sitting-room

Jean (*pointing to the stairs*) That way.

Act II

Ruff Ah, double bluff! All right, I'm going that way. (*He moves towards the stairs*)

Barry, now carrying the moustache, comes charging down the stairs

Barry Glue—glue—must have some glue . . .

Barry pushes into Ruff, sending him sprawling into the swivel chair by the desk, which Jean is holding steady. Jean sits on Ruff's knee, Barry rushes to the bedroom and searches for glue

Jean Oh, dear! Inspector, are you all right?

Ruff pushes her off and the Minister sits on his right knee

Minister Oh, dear! Inspector, are you all right?

Ruff pushes the Minister off

(*Pointing to the bedroom*) That way!
Ruff Wrong. This way, and I'll meet him coming back.

Ruff, with renewed vigour, exits up the main stairs

Jean Glue—glue . . . (*She finds a tube of glue on the desk*)
Barry (*returning to the sitting-room*) Glue—glue . . .
Jean (*pointing to the study*) That way. Hurry.

Barry runs past, taking the glue, and exits to the study.
Ruff suddenly appears down the main stairs as if expecting to catch them out. He looks disappointed

(*Pointing to the bedroom*) That way.

Ruff gives her a look, twitches a little, then goes back the way he came.
Barry enters from the study with the moustache in place

Barry Here we are—the return of Barry Ovis!
Jean (*in sudden horror*) No! Hat! Cravat!

Barry grabs the hat and puts it on. Jean opens the sideboard cupboard and gets his tie and jacket. She puts the tie round his neck and goes to the other side to put the jacket on

Before Jean gets the jacket on, Ruff charges down the bedroom stairs and enters the sitting-room

Jean points to the study, Barry at the floor, the Minister to the main stairs

Barry
Jean } That way. { *Speaking together*
Minister

Ruff looks rather like a stag at bay as he looks from one to the other, twitching badly by now

Barry No, honestly, Inspector. He went through the bedroom window. Dived over.
Ruff Dived over, did he? Head first into the street?
Barry Down the fire-escape.

Ruff looks them up and down, then gives a grim little smile and nod

Ruff Down the fire-escape. That's good. That's good! Because the whole area is cordoned off. If he went that way, one of my men will catch him, won't they? I'll check. I'll check, shall I?

Ruff rams his hat on his head, gives them a wild-eyed look, and exits to the hall

The front door bangs. The Minister regains some of his poise

Minister We might just scrape through so long as he didn't phone my wife in the country to check on Dr Schmuck and Nurse Ruddy Witherspoon. (*To Barry*) You've a lot to learn about lying, Ovis.
Barry Personally, I consider I carried things off with great panache.

Barry turns so that his bottom is down stage and Jean helps him on with his jacket

Minister You don't know your panache from your elbow. We're not out of the wood yet.

The cupboard door bursts open and Potts emerges, triumphant, waving the champagne bottle

Potts No, you're not out of the wood. You're in the fertilizer, my lad—up to your neck!
Minister Potty! What are you doing here?
Potts What am I doing here? What am I doing here? Ha! (*His face suddenly falls. Clearly he has forgotten what he is doing here*) Yes, what *am* I doing here? Why do you have to go and ask? I knew it! One second ago I knew it.
Minister (*with growing hope*) Just a bad dream, Potty.
Potts No, it isn't. I came in here. I went in there. I hid in there. I—*I've got it!*
Minister Damn!
Potts (*triumphantly again*) Yes, my boy, I've got it and I've got *you*.
Minister (*with a hollow laugh*) I don't know what you are talking about.
Potts Shall I tell you what am I talking about? *Crumpet!*
Minister Did you say—*crumpet*?
Potts Yes. Crumpet with a capital C, and capital crumpet, I'll grant you. Let's flush it out, shall we? (*He marches into the bedroom and looks around at the end of the bed*)

The Minister, Barry and Jean follow Potts into the bedroom

Act II

Minister Potts, I'll overlook your monstrous behaviour because of your age and disturbed mental state, but to suggest . . .

The door of the bedroom cupboard opens and Wendy staggers out

Wendy Help, I can't breathe! (*She passes out*)
Potts Crumpet Number One! Come out from under that bed.

Barry and Jean catch Wendy and lay her on the bed. Miss Parkyn crawls out from under the end of the bed

Crumpet Number Two!

Damina crawls out from under the end of the bed. Potts lifts her up

Crumpet Number . . . (*He sees her face for the first time*) Enid!

Damina hangs her head

Damina Grandpa.
Barry } *Grandpa?* { *Speaking*
Minister } { *together*
Potts (*an old man*) But you're at Bognor with the Christian Girls . . .
Damina Well, I had other things to do.
Barry Potty, this is your granddaughter?
Potts It was, but now . . . !
Minister There's a perfectly simple explanation. Carry on, Ovis.
Barry Would you believe it if I told you that I met this lovely child, this modern Florence Nightingale, giving artificial respiration to an old lady who had been struck by lightning on the pavement outside?
Potts No!
Barry Surely that's better than telling you that she'd been messing around with well-known student anarchists and was a prime mover in having me *kidnapped* this morning?
Potts I don't believe it . . .
Barry Of course you don't! *Nobody* would believe a terrible thing like that about any grandchild of yours.
Minister Absolutely not! Well said, Barry! Potty, we may be opposed politically, but I think we both have the welfare of the nation at heart. I'm not going to take advantage of this and I'm sure Ovis will go along with me. As far as we're concerned, the whole thing never happened.
Potts You basta . . .
Minister Don't thank me. Let's go inside and have a drink, shall we? (*Looking under the bed quickly*) Any more crumpet? No! Right! (*He leads the way into the sitting-room*)

The Minister goes into the sitting-room with Barry, Miss Parkyn, Jean and Damina. Potts sits on the side of the bed, stunned

Well done, Barry!

The house telephone rings. The Minister answers

(*Cheerfully*) Hello. Yes? . . . Speaking . . . What! (*He hangs up and turns*

to the others) He's contacted my wife, Birdie. She's on her way up here!
Barry (*in a panic*) Where's the back door?
Minister I haven't got one.
Barry Where would you like one?
Minister Hide, hide, hide.

Miss Parkyn runs into the bedroom, lifts Potts's legs up so that he rolls alongside Wendy and in a daze gets his feet under the sheet, and herself rolls under the bed. Damina follows her. Jean goes to the side of the bed, Barry and the Minister above it. The Minister suddenly points at Jean, who has not been put anywhere

You'd better hide, too!
Jean I don't need to hide...
Minister Yes, you do. You're wearing Birdie's night things!

Jean, too, joins the party under the bed

Barry And Crumpet Number One.

The Minister and Barry lift Wendy off the bed and roll her under it. Potts watches her go, and at the same time eases to the middle of the bed

Make room for one more!
Minister You get out of sight, too.
Barry Yes, indeed! (*He climbs into bed with Potts*)
Minister Now, you leave me to deal with Birdie.
Barry You can't do that! She thinks you're in Glasgow.
Minister Hoots, mon! (*He climbs into the bed on the other side of Potts*)

The Minister and Barry pull the sheet over them, but Potts pushes it down

Potts Help, help, air. I must have air!

Ruff steps through the curtains of the window and stares, slack-jawed, at the bed

CURTAIN

THE CURTAIN CALL

As soon as the CURTAIN falls all the men leave the stage and the girls get out from under the bed and line up with Damina down L, then a gap then Jean then a gap then Miss Parkyn then a gap and then Wendy down R. They bow, and Ruff and Potty come on from the kitchen and behind the bedroom cupboard respectively and come between Damina and Jean and Miss Parkyn and Wendy respectively, bow and step back into line. Barry comes from the stairs in the flat and the Minister from the spiral stairs at the same time, they come C between Jean and Miss Parkyn bow, get into line, smile at each other and bow to the cast and then face front, and they all bow. The CURTAIN falls and rises again, they all bow and it falls and rises once more. This time it stays up and the Caretaker comes on from the L, tormentors carrying the mike on a stand that we have seen before the Town Hall. He puts it in front of Barry and leaves down L. Barry starts to make a speech and after a few words the Minister says, "Excuse me, but it's much easier if you take it off the stand", he does so and holds it in front of Barry who says a few more words and then the mike goes "BLEEP". The Minister stops it bleeping and uses the mike himself, saying, "May I thank you all for coming along, too. Good night." He gives a final "BLEEP" on the mike and cocks a snook at Barry at the same time and the CURTAIN falls. Everybody but Barry and the Minister clear and those two turn up stage and as the CURTAIN rises they walk up stage with the Minister reading the riot act about the mistakes of the night and Barry apologizing. They get to the door C and Barry opens it to carry on apologizing and the Minister pops his head through what should be a solid wall below him. Barry comes back and crosses below the door into the bedroom and the Minister goes through the door and Barry exits up the spiral stairs and the Minister up the flat stairs and the CURTAIN falls for the last time.

FURNITURE AND PROPERTY LIST

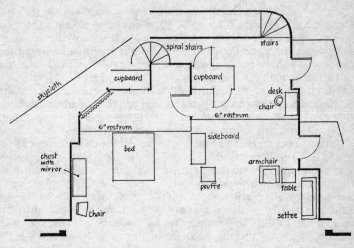

ACT I

Scene 1

On stage: Banquette seat. *On it:* old style record in sleeve
On backcloth: portraits of the Queen and Prince Philip, notice-board, list of Mayors
In flies: Banner with Welcome Message, folds caught up so that it opens wrongly worded

Off stage: Microphone on stand (**Caretaker**)
Duster (**Caretaker**)
Union Jack (**Caretaker**)

Scene 2

On stage: BEDROOM:
Double bed and bedding. *In it:* pair of knickers. *On shelf above:* telephone, lamp
Chest-of-drawers with mirror. *On it:* lamp
Small chair
Built-in cupboard. *In it:* **Barry**'s dressing-gown and pyjamas, morning suit with handkerchief in pocket, Moss Bros case with pair of black shoes and socks, top-hat, cravat, gloves

SITTING-ROOM:
Cupboard: *In it:* broken jug, low stool, golf club, police cape
Low sideboard. *On it:* small TV set, tray with whisky, glasses, jug of water, ashtray, bowl of ice cubes, *Radio Times*, cigars in box, lighter
Pouffe
Armchair
Coffee-table. *On it:* ashtray, telephone. *Under it:* waste-paper basket
Settee. *On it:* 3 toast-racks
Desk. *On it:* lamp, plumbers' brochure, box containing comb and air-freshener, pair of scissors, tube of glue. *Above it:* mirror
Swivel desk chair
On wall: house telephone
Floor and stair carpeting
Window curtains

Off stage: Parcel with toast-rack (**Jean**)
Briefcase and umbrella (**Minister**)
Gladstone bag (**Potts**)
File (**Miss Parkyn**)
Handbag (**Miss Parkyn**)
Truncheon (**Barry**)
Small camera on chain (**Damina**)
Bottle of champagne, pot of caviar, bunch of red roses (**Minister**)
Champagne bucket, flower vase (**Minister**)
2 champagne glasses (**Minister**)
Bunch of keys (**Ruff**)
Whistle (**Minister**)
Torch (**Ruff**)

Personal: **Ruff:** watch, notebook and pencil

ACT II

Off stage: Black vanity bag (**Wendy**)
Brown paper bag with false moustache (**Jean**)
Ham sandwich (**Barry**)
Piece of paper (**Minister**)
File of photographs (**Ruff**)

Personal: **Wendy:** doorkey, wedding-ring

LIGHTING PLOT

Property fittings required: desk lamp, table lamp, bed lamp, brackets in 2 rooms, TV light effect
Interiors. A Town Hall stage; a bedroom and sitting-room

ACT I, SCENE 1

To open: Dim general lighting on stage

Cue 1	**Caretaker** exits with record *Bring up general lighting*	(Page 1)
Cue 2	**Caretaker** signals to limes *Lime on and off in accordance with signals*	(Page 1)
Cue 3	**Barry** gestures to limes *General lighting dims. Lime comes on and moves around according to signals*	(Page 4)
Cue 4	**Barry** does a cutting gesture *Lime off, general lighting up*	(Page 4)

ACT I, SCENE 2. Evening

To open: Stage in darkness

Cue 5	**Jean** switches on lights in sitting-room *Snap on sitting-room brackets and lamp*	(Page 6)
Cue 6	**Jean** switches on television *Fade in TV lighting effect*	(Page 6)
Cue 7	**Minister** switches off television *Fade out TV lighting effect*	(Page 7)
Cue 8	**Jean** switches on the bedroom lights *Snap on bedroom lighting*	(Page 11)
Cue 9	**Barry** switches off bedroom lights *Snap off bedroom lighting*	(Page 13)
Cue 10	**Ruff** switches on bedroom lights *Snap on bedroom lighting*	(Page 14)
Cue 11	**Ruff** switches off bedroom lights *Snap off bedroom lighting*	(Page 15)
Cue 12	**Ruff** switches on bedroom lights *Snap on bedroom lighting*	(Page 16)
Cue 13	**Jean** switches off bedroom lights *Snap off bedroom lighting*	(Page 16)
Cue 14	**Jean** switches on bedroom lights *Snap on bedroom lighting*	(Page 22)

Don't Just Lie There, Say Something!

Cue 15	**Barry** switches off sitting-room lights *Snap off sitting-room lighting*	(Page 23)
Cue 16	**Barry** switches off bedroom lights *Snap off bedroom lighting*	(Page 23)
Cue 17	**Minister** switches on sitting-room lights *Snap on sitting-room lighting*	(Page 23)
Cue 18	**Miss Parkyn** switches on bedroom lights *Snap on bedroom lighting*	(Page 26)
Cue 19	**Miss Parkyn** switches off bedroom lights *Snap off bedroom lighting*	(Page 28)
Cue 20	**Minister** switches off sitting-room lights *Snap off sitting-room lighting*	(Page 29)
Cue 21	**Ruff** switches on bedhead light *Snap on bedhead light and covering spot*	(Page 29)

ACT II. Evening
To open: As close of previous Act

Cue 22	**Ruff** switches on main bedroom lights *Snap on full bedroom lighting*	(Page 30)
Cue 23	**Ruff** switches on sitting-room lights *Snap on sitting-room lighting*	(Page 33)
Cue 24	**Ruff** switches off bedroom lights *Snap off all bedroom lighting*	(Page 34)
Cue 25	**Minister** switches on bedroom lights *Snap on bedroom lighting*	(Page 36)

EFFECTS PLOT

ACT I

Scene 1

Cue 1	**Caretaker** exits with record *After brief pause, start music—"Sweethearts"*	(Page 1)
Cue 2	**Caretaker** exits after dusting *Music replaced by voice; returns at end of speech*	(Page 2)
Cue 3	**Voice:** ". . . Mr Barry Ovis." *Fanfare—alternates with broken starts of Barry's speech*	(Page 2)
Cue 4	**Barry:** "—very lovely girl." *Fanfare*	(Page 2)
Cue 5	**Jean** goes to Barry *Fanfare changes to "Sweethearts" and back*	(Page 3)
Cue 6	**Barry:** ". . . really think of him." *Fanfare*	(Page 3)
Cue 7	**Minister** puts mike on stand *Music—National Anthem, changing to "Sweethearts"*	(Page 5)

Scene 2

Cue 8	**Jean** switches on television *Fade in to announcer's voice*	(Page 6)
Cue 9	**Minister** switches off television *Fade television voice*	(Page 7)
Cue 10	**Minister:** ". . . alcoholic remorse." *Doorbell rings*	(Page 8)
Cue 11	**Minister** exits *Police siren sounds, followed by police whistle*	(Page 11)
Cue 12	**Jean:** ". . . more lies, you mean?" *Doorbell rings*	(Page 14)
Cue 13	**Minister:** ". . . a bloody diesel?" *Doorbell rings*	(Page 24)
Cue 14	**Minister** squirts air-freshener *Doorbell rings*	(Page 24)

ACT II

Cue 15	**Miss Parkyn:** "... instead of Gladys Springs." *Peal of thunder*	(Page 39)
Cue 16	**Barry:** "... a near thing!" *House telephone buzzes*	(Page 57)
Cue 17	**Miss Parkyn** enters from study *Doorbell rings*	(Page 57)
Cue 18	**Minister:** "Not my pigeon." *Doorbell rings*	(Page 57)
Cue 19	**Minister:** "... and stay quiet." *Doorbell rings and continues*	(Page 58)
Cue 20	**Minister:** "Well done, Barry!" *House telephone buzzes*	(Page 65)